Around Us

touchstones

Around Us

edited by

HENRY J. BARON
BRUCE HEKMAN
DANIEL VANDER ARK

The National Union of Christian Schools
William B. Eerdmans Publishing Company
Grand Rapids, Michigan

ISBN 0-8028-1532-4.

HENRY J. BARON received his B.A. from Calvin College, his M.A. from the University of Michigan, and his Ph.D. from the University of Illinois.

Dr. Baron taught in grades 5-12 at Sumas Christian School, Sumas, Washington, and South Christian High School, Grand Rapids, Michigan. He has taught classes at Grand Rapids Junior College, Grand Valley State College, and the University of Illinois and is presently Assistant Professor of English at Calvin College.

Author and editor of several articles, monographs, and curriculum guides, Dr. Baron is director of the *TOUCHSTONES* project and Language Arts Consultant for the National Union of Christian Schools.

BRUCE HEKMAN received his B.A. from Calvin College, his M.A. from the University of Michigan, and his Ph.D. from the University of Illinois.

Dr. Hekman taught at South Christian High School in Grand Rapids, Michigan. He is presently teaching and chairing the English Department at Chicago Christian High School, Palos Heights, Illinois.

Author of several articles and NUCS curriculum publications, Dr. Hekman has also conducted workshops and research in English programs for NUCS secondary schools.

DANIEL VANDER ARK earned his B.A. from Calvin College and his M.A. from the University of Nebraska.

Mr. Vander Ark teaches at Holland Christian High School, where he is chairman of the English Department. He is an author of four of the NUCS nine-week units in high school language arts: *Man and the Outcast, Man and the Search for Self, Man and the Search for Spiritual Significance,* and *Language and Man.*

Editorial services and design were provided by Sandra L. Vander Zicht, NUCS Curriculum Editor, and by Jon Pott, Marlin Van Elderen, Milton Essenburg, and Joel Beversluis of the Wm. B. Eerdmans Publishing Company.

The work presented herein was developed by the NUCS Curriculum Department, supported by a grant from the Christian School Educational Foundation.

CONTENTS

Reflection

PREFACE

TOUCHSTONES began as a revision of *THE PILOT SERIES IN LITERATURE, Book Three,* published by the NUCS in 1964. *TOUCHSTONES'* editors wrote a teacher's guide for *Book Three* in 1970, entitled *Thematic Literature Units 9,* in which they suggested many new selections and a new organizational pattern. This pattern developed the four themes now used in the *TOUCHSTONES* series: "Around Us," "Within Us," "Between Us," and "Above Us." *TOUCHSTONES* incorporates additional new selections, a modified version of the thematic organization, and new photos in a convenient and flexible format.

Underlying this new text is the conviction that curriculum materials should exhibit as equally as possible three major dimensions of Christian education—intellectual, decisional, and creative. We trust that the literature in *TOUCHSTONES* will promote personal growth along these lines. Through the thematic and generic focus in each book, the student can grow intellectually by learning about universal human experiences and concerns and about the artist's craft. As he is caught up in the tensions and conflicts of literature, he can grow in the attitudes and values that so strongly influence basic decisions in life. And he can grow creatively by responding to the literature in his own speaking, writing and acting.

HENRY J. TRIEZENBERG, Ph.D.
NUCS Curriculum Administrator

DONALD OPPEWAL, Ph.D.
NUCS Policy Consultant

PHOTO CREDITS

David Trumbel, p. 3
H. Armstrong Roberts, pp. 5, 36, 79, 153
Harold M. Lambert, pp. 32, 67
© Karsh, Ottawa, from Rapho Guillumette, pp. 80-81
Dave Pott, pp. 88, 117, 150, 184
Steven Friedman, pp. 103, 105, 140-141, 188
James C. Veen Observatory of the Grand Rapids Astronomical Association, Grand Rapids, Michigan, p. 181

ILLUSTRATIONS

Original drawings by Armand Merizon, pp. 19, 55, 63

ACKNOWLEDGMENTS

"Fueled" by Marcie Hans. From *Serve Me a Slice of Moon.* © 1965, by Marcie Hans. Reprinted by permission of Harcourt Brace Jovanovich, Inc.

"Fog" and "Lost," from *Chicago Poems* by Carl Sandburg. Copyright, 1916, by Holt, Rinehart and Winston, Inc.; copyright, 1944, by Carl Sandburg. Reprinted by permission of Harcourt Brace Jovanovich, Inc.

"The Black Hero of the Ranges" by Enos A. Mills. From *St. Nicholas Magazine.* Copyright, 1914, The Century Company. Reprinted by permission of the publishers, Appleton-Century-Crofts, Inc.

"Rat." Reprinted by permission of The Stephen Greene Press from *Animals Nobody Loves,* © 1971 by Ronald Rood.

"An Introduction to Dogs," from *Family Reunion* by Ogden Nash. Copyright 1938 by Ogden Nash. Used by permission of Little, Brown and Company.

"Catalog" by Rosalie Moore. Reprinted by permission. Copyright © 1940, 1968 The New Yorker Magazine, Inc.

"l)a" by e.e. cummings. © 1958 by e.e. cummings. Reprinted from his volume *95 Poems* by permission of Harcourt Brace Jovanovich, Inc.

"Dandelions" by Will Stanton. Copyright © 1960 by The New Yorker Magazine, Inc.

"The Sloth" copyright 1950 by Theodore Roethke, "The Meadow Mouse" copyright © 1963 by Beatrice Roethke, Administratrix of the Estate of Theodore Roethke. From the book *Collected Poems of Theodore Roethke.* Reprinted by permission of Doubleday and Company, Inc.

"Explosion," from the poem "Days," from *As If: Poems New and Selected* by John Ciardi. Copyright by the Press of Rutgers College in New Jersey. Reprinted by permission of the author; and of Rutgers University Press.

"The Whistle Blows," from *Brave Men* by Ernie Pyle. Copyright 1943, 1944 by Scripps-Howard Newspaper Alliance. Copyright

1944 by Ernie Pyle. Copyright © 1971, 1972 by Holt, Rinehart and Winston, Inc. Reprinted by permission of Holt, Rinehart and Winston, Inc.

"Disabled" by Wilfred Owen. From *The Collected Poems of Wilfred Owen*, edited by C. Day Lewis. Copyright Chatto & Windus, Ltd. 1946, © 1963. Reprinted by permission of the Estate of the late Harold Owen; Chatto & Windus, Ltd.; and the New Directions Publishing Corporation.

"Peril from the Sky," from "Air Pollution: Peril from the Skies," from *Senior Scholastic*. © 1969 by Scholastic Magazines, Inc.

"Rock Bottom" by Lorenz Graham. From *Directions 2*, by John Durham, Lorenz Graham, and Elsa Graser. Houghton Mifflin Company, 1972. Reprinted by permission.

"Who's Who?" Copyright 1945 by W. H. Auden. From *Collected Shorter Poems 1927-1957* by W. H. Auden. Reprinted by permission of Random House, Inc.; and Faber & Faber Ltd.

"The Coming of the Teacher," from *The Story of My Life* by Helen Keller. Published by Doubleday and Company, Inc.

"Unwanted" by Edward Field. From *Stand Up, Friend, with Me*. Copyright © 1963 by Edward Field. Reprinted by permission of Grove Press, Inc.

"Carlozini," from pp. 178-180 in *House Made of Dawn* by N. Scott Momaday. Copyright © 1966, 1967, 1968 by N. Scott Momaday. Reprinted by permission of Harper & Row Publishers, Inc.

"A Name on the Wall" by Robert Marmorstein. From *The University Review* (June, 1965). Reprinted by permission of the University of Missouri-Kansas City.

"Miss Brill." Copyright 1922 by Alfred A. Knopf, Inc. and renewed 1950 by J. Middleton Murry. From *The Short Stories of Katherine Mansfield* by Katherine Mansfield. Reprinted by permission of Alfred A. Knopf, Inc.; and The Society of Authors as the literary representative of the Estate of Katherine Mansfield.

"Ex-Basketball Player," from *The Carpentered Hen and Other Tame Creatures* by John Updike. Copyright © 1957 by John Updike. Originally appeared in *The New Yorker*. By permission of Harper & Row, Publishers, Inc.

"The Miner," from "The Miner" by Maxwell Bodenheim. Reprinted by permission of Liveright Publishers, New York.

"The Market Man," from *A Remembered Darkness* by John Ratti. Copyright © 1964 by John Ratti. All rights reserved. Reprinted by permission of The Viking Press, Inc.

"Shane," pp. 1-15, omitting pp. 12-13, from the novel *Shane* by Jack Schaefer. Copyright © 1949 by Jack Schaefer. Copyright © 1954 by John McCormack. Reprinted by permission of Houghton Mifflin Company.

"Let Me Tell You about My Ma" by Marinus Swets. From *The Banner* (May 12, 1972). Reprinted by permission.

"A Mother in Mannville." Reprinted by permission of Charles Scribner's Sons from *When the Whippoorwill* by Marjorie Kinnan Rawlings. Copyright 1940 Marjorie Kinnan Rawlings.

"Sunday Morning," "Royalty," and "A Song for Simplicity." Reprinted from *Listen to the Green* by Luci Shaw. © 1971 by Harold Shaw Publishers, Box 567, Wheaton, IL 60187. Used by permission.

"Foul Shot" by Edwin Hoey. Special permission granted by *Read* magazine, published by Xerox Education Publications. © Xerox Corp. 1962.

"The Base Stealer." Copyright © 1948 by Robert Francis. Reprinted from *The Orb Weaver* by Robert Francis, by permission of Wesleyan University Press.

"To Look at Any Thing" by John Moffitt. © 1961 by John Moffitt. Reprinted from his volume *The Living Seed* by permission of Harcourt Brace Jovanovich, Inc.

"Traveling through the Dark," in *Traveling through the Dark*, by William Stafford. Copyright © 1960 by William Stafford. By permission of Harper & Row, Publishers, Inc.

"Interlude III." Copyright 1944 by Karl Shapiro. Reprinted from *Selected Poems* by Karl Shapiro, by permission of Random House, Inc.

"On a Squirrel Crossing the Road in Autumn, in New England," from *Collected Poems 1930-1960* by Richard Eberhart. © 1960 by Richard Eberhart. Reprinted by permission of Oxford University Press, Inc.; and Chatto & Windus, Ltd.

TO THE STUDENT

Your world surrounds you.

Much of it is fascinating. Maybe you remember how as a small child you would often make a spectacular discovery and cry, "Look Mom, look at the pretty flower I found!" and hold up a dandelion before Mom's unappreciative eyes. Or you would spy a highly polished pebble and excitedly exclaim: "Dad, come quick and look at the shiny rock I found. I think it's a rare one!" It wasn't, of course, but it was exciting to think so for a moment.

Much of the world is also puzzling and sometimes painful. As you grow older you become more thoughtful about that aspect of the world, and the exclamations of earlier days tend to give way to such queries as:

> I wonder how that old man became paralyzed.
>
> Do you suppose an eagle actually feels superior to a sparrow?
>
> Did you notice the look on that old lady's face when those kids laughed at her funny hat?
>
> Did you ever feel close to God because you felt close to nature?

Yes, your world is all around you. And when you stop to look at it closely, you find not only much that delights you, but also much that puzzles and frightens and angers you.

This book is about all those things. In it are poems and stories, photographs and illustrations that provide a special way of seeing many of the familiar but also some unfamiliar parts of your surrounding world.

You will find the seeing interesting and worthwhile, for learning to see more is often also to grow more. And what your surrounding world needs is your growing awareness and appreciation of it, as well as your growing concern and sense of responsibility for it.

Enjoy your reading and seeing!

HENRY J. BARON
Project Director

Observation

Something in the wild cherry—
the cat or another caution—
triggers the starlings and the tree
explodes. Who would have thought
so many pieces of life in one tree?
"Explosion"

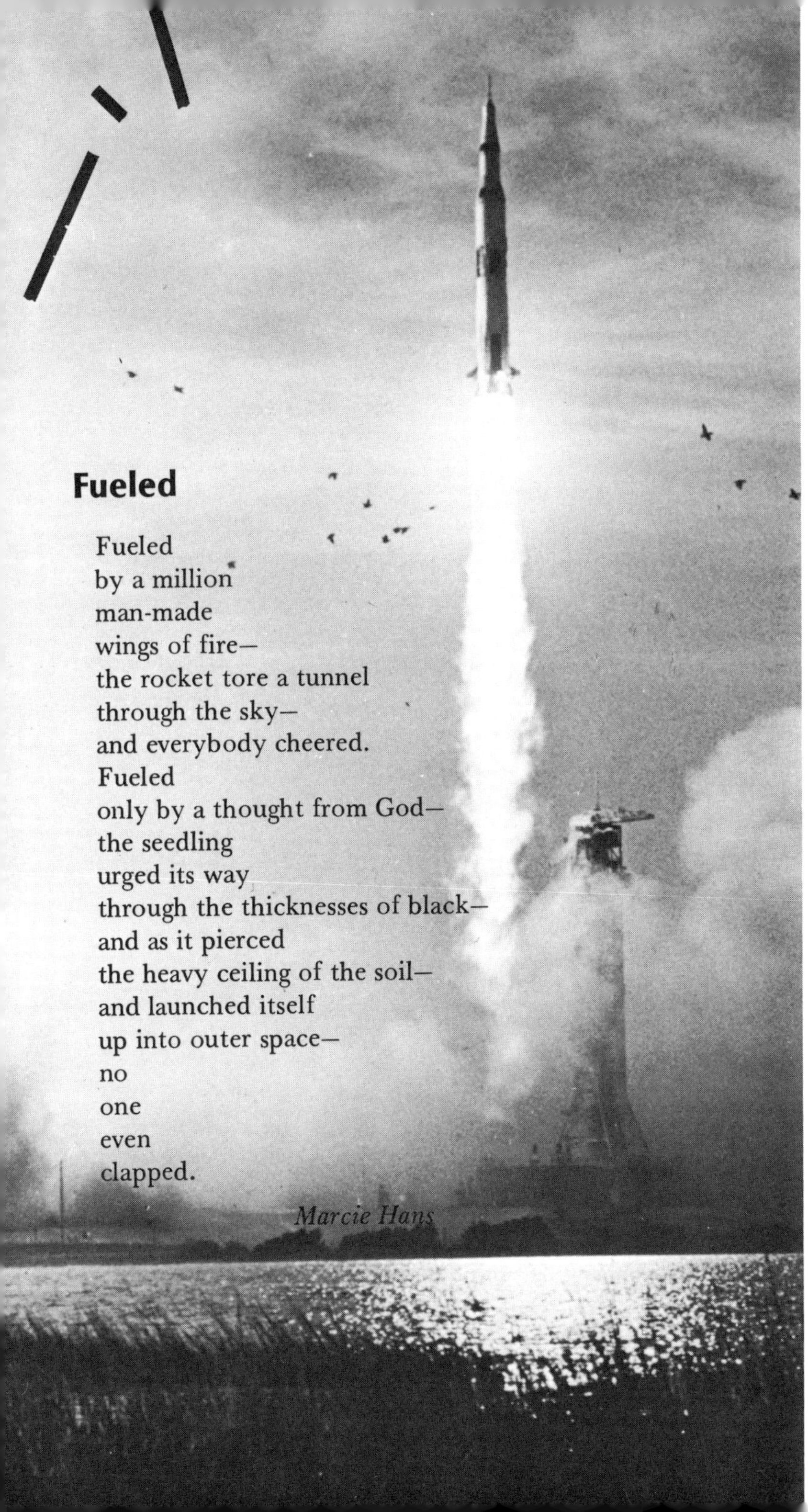

Fueled

Fueled
by a million
man-made
wings of fire–
the rocket tore a tunnel
through the sky–
and everybody cheered.
Fueled
only by a thought from God–
the seedling
urged its way
through the thicknesses of black–
and as it pierced
the heavy ceiling of the soil–
and launched itself
up into outer space–
no
one
even
clapped.

Marcie Hans

Fog

The fog comes
on little cat feet.

It sits looking
over harbor and city
on silent haunches
and then moves on.

Carl Sandburg

Smog

 The smog comes
On huge dragon claws.

 It stands breathing
Over ghetto and suburb
  waiting to move
 But it lingers on.

A Student

Which poem uses the most appropriate comparison?

Lost

Desolate and lone
All night long on the lake
Where fog trails and mist creeps,
The whistle of a boat
Calls and cries unendingly,
Like some lost child
In tears and trouble
Hunting the harbor's breast
And the harbor's eyes.

Carl Sandburg

The Black Hero of the Ranges

Enos A. Mills

"One thousand dollars reward for the man who captures the black stallion, the terror of the range!" But not a man in Nevada could get near enough to drop his rope on this wonderful animal. Read what happened when the riders of Diamond H ranch went on an organized hunt to capture him.

The pungent odor of the campfire drifted down the swale and carried with it the savory smell of the cooking supper. All afternoon the Diamond H riders had been arriving; word had been passed that a feast would be spread at sundown in honor of the owner of the Diamond H ranch, who had arrived for his first visit to the ranch in three years.

The riders had all arrived but young Hank—he of the shiny spurs and new "chaps." No rider in the outfit possessed such complete trappings. Though Hank was not a regular puncher, it pleased him mightily to be called one. He was a kind of messenger-boy for the outfit and rode far and wide carrying orders from the foreman or going down to the post for the mail. When in camp, he assisted the cook, a task he detested as being beneath his dignity. But Hank was proud of the Diamond H and boasted that no ranch in Nevada had such riders and ropers.

The feast was nearing the end in the soft dusk of evening, when Hank charged down upon the scene at a reckless gallop and stopped abruptly within the circle of the firelight.

The foreman straightened up with observing eye upon the foaming horse. "Didn't I tell you not to run Old Baldy any more?"

Every cowpuncher eyed Hank, and several tried to divert the foreman by witty remarks and laughter.

But Hank did not wither under the accusation.

"I had a try at the black stallion," he observed, as he fixed his eyes on the owner.

"Where?" came a half-dozen demands at once. "Where?" rapped out the owner. It was like an explosion in their midst. The feast was scattered, and instantly there was a stampede of talk. Each rider was possessed of the same thought—to capture that wonderful steed that had so long led his herd whither he would, defying capture, daring to go where no horse ever had gone before, and upon whose head was set a price.

"I thought you said the black stallion never came down from the rough country?" The owner waited eagerly for the foreman's answer.

"It's the first time he's shown up down here since we had the chase after him two years ago."

"Jess, I'd like to have that horse, and I'm willing to go to any amount of trouble to get him. But the question is, can we?"

The foreman looked into the fire and ran his hands thoughtfully through his hair. At length he turned to the owner. "I believe we've got the best chance at him, now that he's left the rough country, that we've ever had. He's an old fox, though, and there's nothing he doesn't know about being chased. It's about as easy to round up a bird as to try to corner him. Still, the water's all gone, higher up, and he's got to range down here. If we only had more men and a mustang outfit, I believe we could–" The owner's heavy hand reached the foreman's shoulder and stopped him midway of the prediction.

"Get the men and the outfit. I'll foot the bills. If you get him, I'll hand you a year's salary. You can promise the men whatever reward you like, but the thing is, *get that horse!*"

Hank moved opposite the two men and leaned forward across the embers of the fire.

"Where did you see him, Hank?"

"About three miles up the valley by the spring. There were twenty in the herd he was leading."

"All right, Hank; get a fresh horse and ride down to the post and pick up every rider you can. Find old Sam Higler, and tell him he's to be here with his canvas corral outfit by tomorrow night. Tell every one you see that the black's come down, and there's a reward of a thousand dollars for the man who drops his rope on him and brings him in." Hank vanished in the direction of the rope corral and five minutes later was riding rapidly toward the post. After he had gone, the owner turned to the foreman. "Jess," said he, "did I ever tell you where the stallion came from?" The foreman's interested face invited him to proceed.

"It was five years ago that a Syrian peddler was killed by a couple of halfbreeds because he had this wonderful black stallion. The Indians took the horse clear across the desert to make their escape, but just when they were about to sell him, the stallion killed one and lamed the other with his heels and got away. It was not long before he appeared with a wild-horse herd, and since then he's been the terror of the range; and there's not a man in Nevada who can boast of ever getting near enough to drop his rope on him. I doubt if he's ever taken alive. Before I quit the ranch three years ago, I'd ridden in a couple of chases after him, and I tell you he's got sense and legs that can put him over a hundred miles any day."

They sat in silence, each looking into the embers of the fire.

Twenty Diamond H riders surrounded the valley early in the morning and from the passes looked down at the wild-horse band led by the big black stallion. It was a long, narrow valley, and the eastern wall had but a single pass where anything but winged creatures could escape. At the upper end the valley narrowed, and leading down into it was an old, timeworn pass; here were posted three men with as many extra horses. West of the valley, the ridge rose abruptly. In ten miles it had only five breaks, where steep canyons penetrated its rocky top and broke the barrier. At each break two men posted themselves and waited. They gained these passes by circuitous routes. The lower end of the valley was guarded by three men, who lounged about, allowing their horses to graze.

At noon Hank arrived upon a jaded horse, and singly or by twos and threes the other punchers came in during the afternoon, each mounted on his best horse and with carefully coiled ropes. At dark, Sam Higler put in an appearance with his mustang trap, which was set up overnight across the lower end of the valley. This trap consisted of a brown canvas twelve feet high, which represented an impassable wall. Near the center the wall curved sharply, making a natural corner with an inviting opening leading into a canvas corral beyond. It was a cunning contrivance, and in it scores of wild mustangs had been captured. It was here that they hoped to capture the famous stallion.

Extra men were sent to reinforce the guards at all the passes. Fifteen of the best ropers were kept at camp, and these were to take part at the finish of the chase.

From the main ranch there had been sent up a dozen thoroughbred, long-legged, racing horses, which were to be used in case the stallion broke through the barrier and escaped from the valley or were to be held in reserve until the chase had tired out the crafty leader. Then they were to appear suddenly from behind the canvas wall and go after the herd like the wind.

Orders were to shoot the stallion if he broke through the lines. The rest of the herd was worth four thousand dollars, and their addition to the ranch stock would be valuable.

The only ones at breakfast at the chuck wagon that morning were the owner, the foreman, and Hank. While the men settled the final details of the chase, Hank tidied up the camp things and saddled his horse.

"Hank, one of the boys rode back yesterday to report that there's still a little water at the muddy spring water hole." Hank was silent; sudden fear had chilled him. The foreman continued: "If the foxy old stallion gets away from us in the valley, that's the only place in a hundred miles he can get water; and I guess after we've run him a hundred miles or so, he'll be wanting water, too. You'd better ride up to the muddy spring, Hank, and stick it out there until dark. There's no telling what may happen today, but whatever comes, the chase will end at dark."

Hank turned away, blinking fast and swallowing hard. His hopes of riding with the foreman and the owner were thus suddenly blasted, leaving behind a sense of revolt that fairly hurt. After discovering the horse, he would lose all the excitement of the chase.

Soon after daylight the foreman and the owner rode into the valley above the canvas wall. They galloped easily toward the spring where Hank had seen the horses two days before. When they rounded a knoll a half mile below the water hole, they sighted the wonderful stallion on guard on a slight elevation, with the herd feeding quietly below. Instantly the band was off up the valley, and the foreman was riding rapidly in pursuit. The owner stopped at the spring, where he would wait until the time came for the concerted dash and capture of the big black. It was a waiting game, and patience was to play an important part.

Ten miles up the valley, straight for the steep trail at the upper end, swept the black leader at the head of his herd. But a quarter of a mile from the pass he stopped, wheeled, and doubled back. The foreman was riding near the western wall, and the band passed him on its return trip without being forced into too close quarters.

One of the men on guard at the pass dashed down with a fresh horse, and five minutes later the foreman was after the herd again with the second horse. He galloped along a half mile behind the stallion, and not once did he press the chase or excite the band unduly.

At the sight of the brown canvas wall barring his way, the stallion spun around and fled wildly up the valley again. But three of the others went straight on through the narrow opening at the center and were easy victims in the canvas corral. On another fresh horse the foreman continued the chase. Not once did he come nearer than the half mile, and never did he permit the band to stop for more than a minute or two at a time.

When within a quarter of a mile of the pass, the stallion again scented danger and again wheeled back down the valley. Once more a man dashed out from hiding with a fresh horse, and the chase continued. It was settling down now to one of dogged endurance, with the odds against the stallion. Fresh horses were in plenty for the foreman, but the wonderful black kept on, hour after hour, leading his dwindling band with what seemed tireless energy. Ceaselessly they kept him moving. Three round trips of the valley, sixty miles, and ten of his mates were out of the chase, and before the fourth round of the valley was finished, they were dropping out rapidly, being roped and dragged in submission to the canvas corral.

Frequently now the stallion would stop and watch until his relentless pursuer was within a hundred yards; then he would be off again. His black coat was covered with foam; he was becoming uncertain on his feet and stumbled often. He approached the water hole, but it was guarded. Wearily he turned back down the valley because it was easier going.

The foreman fired three quick signal shots, and from behind the brown canvas wall rode the best ropers of the region, mounted on the fleetest horses. The stallion slowed his flight and went on down the valley along the western side. The riders waited across the valley until he had passed, then they spread out across the level floor.

Ten abreast, and absolutely certain of success, they galloped easily along behind the stallion as he went on straight toward the canvas barrier. They did not hurry; there was no need; an easy gallop kept pace with the stallion's now unsteady gait.

A hundred yards from the barrier, he wheeled defiantly. Facing them, he waited. The foreman shouted an order, and they dashed wildly forward, each eager to be first to drop his rope over the wary head and win eternal fame in the region as the subduer of the most wonderful horse in Nevada.

With heaving sides and flaming eyes the stallion waited their coming. When the nearest riders were fifty feet away, he charged directly toward them, getting into his full stride in spite of his weariness, and by the time he reached them, he was going at top speed. His unexpected charge threw the riders into confusion. Their racing horses were not trained to the roping game like their cow horses; besides, each rider was racing wildly, and each had his full length of rope ready for a long cast in order to be first.

Straight between two riders went the stallion. The men were alert and active in spite of their mounts. They made casts at the same instant, and their ropes met in mid-air above his head. One loop dropped short, and the other was so large that he leaped half through before the man could snake the slack with a quick backward jerk of his hand and tighten up. Even then, his horse was broadside when the plunging stallion reached the end of the rope with a tremendous charge that lifted the racer clear of his feet and flung him violently to the ground.

To save himself, the man instinctively let go the rope, which he had snubbed around the saddle horn, and at the stallion's first lunge it slipped from the saddle and went trailing off behind the black. Three leaps more, and it dropped harmlessly to the ground. The stallion was free again.

The very number of his pursuers was his advantage. A hundred feet away the side of the valley rose at half pitch, and rough rocks and dense scrub were scattered thickly up the slope. Up he went over ragged rock slabs, forcing his way through the scrub where no ridden horse could follow.

Straight up the mountain the great horse fought his way, though it was strewn with huge blocks of bare rock piled in a forbidding mass of debris. The route looked impossible.

"Don't shoot! He's all in," ordered the foreman. From above came the shouts of the men guarding the pass: "Let him come! We'll get him."

Desperately the men below tried to follow, and impatiently the men at the top waited and watched his slow upward progress. They straightened their ropes, tightened their cinches, and made sure that every detail was ready. Behind them, back of the ridge top, lay a narrow plateau, and beyond rose a second ridge. Upon this level bench they would capture the famous stallion and the reward.

A hundred feet from the top, the stallion doubled back, leaped boldly over a narrow chasm, and followed along a narrow ledge of bare rock that ran along the face of the cliff. It was barely wide enough for him to edge along, and there was every chance that it might pinch out.

But the ledge did not pinch out, and the stallion came to the end of it fifty yards farther, where a section of the barrier had gone out with the rock slice. Up over the rock slabs the horse fought his mad way, always toward the top. His progress was slow and painful. Often he was minutes gaining a few feet. Still nothing daunted or defeated him. The men watching from above laughed, exulted at the sight.

A narrow rock-filled gully ran back across the plateau toward the ridge beyond. Scrub growth filled in between the rocks. It was to the mouth of this gully that the horse finally forced his way.

The men were waiting for him on foot. Each dropped his rope over the coveted head with a yell of triumph.

No sooner did the ropes tighten upon the stallion's neck than he became an explosion of action. Up the slope toward the level ground he charged, and the men, confident of success, let him go.

Once in the open, they stopped him by throwing their weight against their ropes. With flaming eyes, mouth open, and ears laid flat, the stallion came down at them, a terrible monster of rage.

The horse was within ten feet of the men, when one of them let go his rope and dived aside as the black bulk lurched by. The other threw his weight against his rope, and the stallion turned upon him with bared teeth and awful, flashing eyes. He saved himself only by leaping blindly into the scrub in the gully.

When the men recovered their feet, they rushed to their horses and were after the runaway pell-mell. But the stallion continued along the broken top of the ridge, where it seemed as if he would surely tumble headlong back into the valley. He dared every obstacle for liberty, leaped treacherous gaps in the rock barrier where his enemies dared not follow, and made his way across fields of huge, broken rocks where no other horse had ever dared.

On the level the fresh horses of the men could easily have overtaken him; but among the rocks and chasms of the ridge top, they had difficulty in keeping him in sight. Their horses were not fighting a life-and-death battle and could not follow the way the stallion went. They had to make detours where the black forged straight up the slope.

Seeing that he was about to gain the second ridge top,

the men opened on him with their six-shooters, but he plunged desperately into the growth of scrub just back of the second ridge top and went crashing headlong out of sight, and safe from the spiteful guns.

Ten minutes after the stallion disappeared into the scrub, the men reached the top of the ridge and saw the plain trail where he had entered the thicket. They separated and started circling around the copse in opposite directions, chagrined at their failure either to capture or kill the wonderful black horse. They rode desperately to intercept him when he should emerge from the far side of the sheltering growth. But as soon as they were out of hearing, the crafty animal came out at the spot where he had entered the thicket and started westward along the rough ridge top. Sometimes he stopped for a moment to rest, and always he watched the back trail. When he went on again, he followed the roughest way he could find.

An hour later, the men from the valley came up and found his tracks, which told once more how the big black stallion had won his freedom. In the second valley they found where he had joined another wild-horse band. But they knew he would soon leave the band and seek shelter; so they scattered and began careful search for tracks near every thicket. They hoped to find him before he had sufficiently rested to run away from them.

It was a game for life and freedom by the stallion, and he never gave up. Leaving the wild herd abruptly, he rested a few minutes, then pushed on to a hiding place. But he allowed little time for rest; always he went on and on, putting as much distance between himself and his enemies as his strength would permit. Thus it was he worked his way to the lonely water hole.

Through all the long hours, Hank waited at the

muddy spring beside it. While he kept lonely vigil, his heart welled up against the foreman and the others. He almost hoped that the stallion would get away. Surely the chase was over, long since, for the sun was dropping low. However, his orders were to wait until dark, and he would stick it out. Not because he cared what any of them thought or said or did, but because he was a boy—and almost a man. They had not given him a fair chance, and he knew that they would give the stallion even less.

At four in the afternoon Hank unsaddled Old Baldy, hobbled him, and allowed him to graze away from the spring. Behind a scrub where the sand had drifted, he scooped out a hole with his hands, and snuggled in the bottom with his six-shooter within touch. Long rides, loss of sleep, and constant vigil had wearied him more than he knew. In five minutes he was asleep. The sun touched the distant mountains and sank slowly behind them.

A wild snort awakened him, and he started up stupidly, half awake, gun in hand. He arose cautiously. Thirty feet away stood the stallion, legs braced wide apart to keep from falling, muscles all aquiver. He was reeking with foam and dirt. But his eyes were blazing with that terrible fear and hate of man. The breeze carried the man smell away from the stallion, and undersized Hank, standing knee-deep in the sandpit, did not look formidable.

For a moment they faced each other across the water hole, each immovable with surprise. Instinctively Hank's gun hand crept out and rose slowly in front, sliding out toward the stallion. He covered a foam fleck between the blazing eyes, held the gun steady there for a second; then he lowered it. "He can't get away anyhow," he said aloud.

At the sound of his voice, the stallion pulled himself together with a jerk. Plainly, though, he was at the end of his race. He must have water or perish. Slowly he advanced. A few steps from the spring he halted; his instinct warned him against nearer approach to his hated enemy. But he was too weak to run away, and, after hesitating, he staggered forward and dropped to his knees at the water hole.

"All right, old fellow, you win!" and Hank replaced his gun in its holster and stood watching as the horse buried his nose in the muddy water and drank in great, sobbing gulps, until the water hole was empty. Hank was glad he had dug it out in the morning. The little hole held perhaps two buckets of dark water, but it made only a taste for the stallion.

"Looks like they'd given you a run for your life, old fellow," and Hank moved forward slowly, continued talking, and edging nearer. Soothingly he talked his way forward while the horse held his hot muzzle pressed against the wet sand, eagerly sucking up the water as it flowed slowly forth. Its slowness made him impatient, and he began pawing wildly.

"Now don't do that!" Hank chided; "don't you see you've filled up the hole?"

Far back in his mind, the stallion must have remembered that men *had* been kind to him; for he was not afraid now of this first man-being who had been kind to him since he escaped the Indians. There was something in the gentle touch of the boy that thrilled him with vague memories. He waited patiently while with bare hands Hank scooped out the water hole.

Tears were streaming down Hank's boyish face as he loosened the two ropes and tossed them aside. Patting the foam-flecked neck, he talked on and on. The horse waited impatiently for the water that came so maddeningly slow. After his second draft, he nosed Hank and whinnied eagerly.

Darkness settled unnoticed. Suddenly the stallion lifted his head, alert, and looked intently toward the east, ears pricked sharply forward and alarm in his manner. Hank could see or hear nothing, but he watched the revived horse keenly. A moment later came distant hoofbeats, and the stallion galloped stiffly away into the darkness.

Soon the rough voice of a man greeted Hank as he stood motionless by the water hole.

"Hello, fellows! Did you get him?" Hank's question saved him from having to answer that question himself and conveyed to the men exactly what he wished it to. He had scooped out a hole in the sand, tossed the ropes into it, and smoothed the sand over them.

Hank was silent on the homeward ride. His heart was filled with conflicting emotions, and he heard only part of the talk about the daredevil horse that had climbed rock walls and fought for his freedom. It seemed to be the general opinion that the stallion had joined another band.

Fifteen miles across the rough country Hank rode every Saturday afternoon. He had asked, then demanded, of the foreman this half holiday, and had at last secured it through strategy. In his pockets were lumps of sugar, offerings of salt, bread, and other treats for the stallion. Twice during the first month he had sighted the wonderful black and had coaxed him to approach and accept the offerings he had brought to cement their friendship. If the stallion failed to keep the tryst, Hank would return to the ranch dejected and morose.

It was near roundup time, and some extra work had delayed Hank past his usual starting time. He did not take the precaution of starting off and circling back to throw the others off his trail, but took a short cut up the valley, climbed the steep trail at its upper end, and emerged through the pass that overlooked the muddy spring. He went down the opposite slope at a rapid pace. Baldy had once been a famous cow horse, but had grown too old for active service. They were going down the smooth slope like the wind, when Baldy stepped into a hole and plunged downward, turning completely over in his fall. Hank was flung from the saddle, but one foot stuck in its stirrup. Then he lost consciousness.

Pain in his leg roused him after a few minutes, and he sat up, dazed.

Noticing that his right toe was twisted in, he tried to reach out to it, but his hand refused to obey the summons—his collarbone was injured, too. His head cleared, and he realized what had happened. Baldy lay with his head doubled under his body; his neck was broken.

Hank crawled painfully to his saddle and cut the thongs that bound his slicker. Out of it, with his left hand, he cut strips and slowly bound the throbbing ankle and made a sling for his useless arm. When he had finished his bandaging, he started crawling slowly toward the spring. On one hand and both knees he dragged himself along, stopping often to rest.

The stallion snorted at the strange crawling object and circled until he got the wind; the smell convinced him, and he decided to venture nearer. Sitting quiet, Hank coaxed, gave sugar sparingly, and a little salt too. When the stallion was used to his new appearance, he pressed firmly with his left hand behind the horse's knees. "Lie down, lie down, lie down," he begged, but the black horse did not understand and edged away.

Water at the hole revived Hank, but at times during the night he was half delirious, calling out for the stallion to come to him; and all night the stallion kept vigil about the spring. Frequently at the call he would approach and nose the boy, whinny eagerly, and walk round and round him.

At daylight the great black horse was still waiting beside the boy. Sometimes Hank would rouse himself with an effort and try to get the horse to lie down. Toward noon Hank's head cleared, and he crawled slowly to an upthrust of rock and coaxed the stallion to him. With a painful effort he dragged himself upon the mighty back, and turned the stallion's head toward the ranch. They traveled slowly. Many times the rider reeled recklessly and came near tumbling off. At such times the horse would stop and wait until Hank gave the word to go on again.

Fifteen cowpunchers were lolling away Sunday afternoon in the shade of the bunkhouse. Hank's absence was being discussed. Around a point two hundred yards away came the stallion. At the sight of the men he stopped quickly, and Hank narrowly saved himself from pitching headlong to the ground.

The stallion turned his head and looked at Hank. "It's all right, old fellow; I'll see you through. Go on!" And the horse went forward at an easy pace, with Hank clinging with his left hand tightly to the flowing mane.

Fifteen punchers held the attitude they were in when the horse appeared—they were frozen with astonishment. Not one of them broke the silence nor moved a hand.

At the gate the stallion stopped, and Hank crumpled into the arms of one of the punchers, and then to the ground. He lay quiet so long that the horse gently pawed at him and whinnied anxiously. "I'm all right, old pal," Hank said aloud, through clenched teeth. "You hit the trail; I'll see you again, when I'm able to travel."

With head and tail high, mane flowing in the breeze, the stallion galloped away, swinging his magnificent head from side to side as he went and looking backward continually.

But not a man stirred.

What would you have done in Hank's situation and for what reasons?

The place in a story where the struggle reaches a turning point—the moment of greatest interest—is known as the *climax.* What is the climax, or moment of greatest interest, in "The Black Hero of the Ranges"?

Rat

Ronald Rood

Rats!

They fought the dogs and killed the cats,
And bit the babies in the cradles,
And ate the cheeses out of the vats,
And licked the soup from the cooks' own ladles,
Split open the kegs of salted sprats,
Made nests inside men's Sunday hats,
And even spoiled the women's chats
By drowning their speaking
With shrieking and squeaking
In fifty different sharps and flats.
Robert Browning, *The Pied Piper of Hamelin*

There are hundreds of books and articles telling what a fine creature the rat is. Really.

The trouble with these stories is that they are nearly all shelved in sterile laboratories or in the stacks of medical libraries. They languish, scarcely read by any but professional researchers, between the covers of magazines with ho-hum titles like *Animal Physiology,* the *Journal of Heredity* or *Biological Abstracts.*

Further, these accounts are so muffled in awkward,

stilted language ("three of the test subjects evidenced fibrovascular recession, giving a neo-classic example of the Glommus Syndrome") that most such recitals have a short synopsis at the end of the article so you can tell what really happened. Nevertheless and despite any gobbledygook, those reports tell an amazing story.

They show how *Rattus norvegicus*—the common brown, or Norway, rat—has come to the service of mankind through the years. In these accounts he is wearing an immaculate white laboratory smock, but he is merely an albino variant of that creature that pokes through the rubbish at the dump or scuttles out of your way in an alley. Rattus the Scientist and Rattus the Scavenger are one and the same creature.

Much of what we've learned about heredity has been taught us by the rat. We understand our own behavior better after watching that of our pink-eyed, white-coated, four-footed teacher. Many a medical career has been launched after a squint at the fascinating innards of a white rat in a school biology lab. Cancer, arthritis, heart disease—to name just a few—are maladies whose comeuppance may depend largely on the laboratory rat. He has already done his stint in the wars on polio and tuberculosis, and has tried out such delights as zero gravity and high-G forces in the space program.

We owe him a great debt, which we can repay by demanding humane conditions for, and handling of, all living creatures used in scientific experiments, for much of our civilization rests on the narrow shoulders of this durable little rodent.

On the other hand, a great deal of our modern world is in danger of being toppled by the same creature. Here we meet our Dr. Jekyll when he is being the infamous Mr. Hyde. He's dressed in inconspicuous brown, thus blending in with almost any situation, especially under cover of darkness. Those same chisel-teeth that have taught us about minerals and vitamins are busy gnawing away at the very house we live in. If that house caves in, the rat will suffer too, for this one-pound nuisance is at his pesky best where human beings are at their worst: in crowded slums, dingy hovels and dirty waterfronts. A common rat abandoned in the woods or out in the meadow is out of its element. It quickly makes its way to the nearest habitation of man, its biggest friend and greatest enemy.

Fleas carried by rats were responsible for the grim toll of bubonic plague during the Dark Ages. Murine typhus, the scourge of war, is spread by their lice. Estimates of damage to all kinds of material–food, textiles, lumber–vary tremendously, but the U.S. Fish and Wildlife Service says that every man, woman and child in the nation pays nearly two dollars a year in direct losses due to rats, whether they ever see a rat or not.

Yet you've got to hand it to him. In a world that has seen the tragic loss of the passenger pigeon, the great auk and the Carolina parakeet almost within the memory of people now living, the brown rat has flourished. In spite of traps and cats and poisons and campaigns, we still have rats aplenty. Again, estimates vary widely, but it's thought that there is at least one rat for each person alive in the world today. That's about five billion of the rodents. Eight thousand new rats–and people–are being produced every hour. Not bad, when you get down to it, for an animal that nobody wants.

How can the common rat do so well over the centuries? Why did it survive while the splendid Steller sea cow–a marine goliath twice the size of a walrus–was completely wiped out two decades after being discovered on a North Sea island? What kindly providence protected the rats on the ships of the sailors who sought the eggs and flesh of the last dodo?

The answer lies in the rat's ability to adjust to new situations. It can fit in almost anywhere. The Norway rat got its name from its occurrence on sailing vessels, with the busy maritime nation of Norway getting the credit. Actually the animal probably originated in Asia. It spread from one port to another as shipping flourished in the eighteenth century, apparently crossing the Atlantic about the time of the American Revolution. Here it tunneled its way through cellars and under wharves. The smaller black rat (*Rattus rattus*)—also an ocean voyager—took the other half of man's habitation, becoming the "roof rat" until gradually driven out by its more aggressive cousin.

Not only can rats go almost anywhere, but they can eat nearly anything they find when they get there. Almost any plant or animal food will do—plus some things that aren't food at all. Rats chew through heavy lead shielding on power cables. They chip away at old, crumbly concrete. They've been known to gnaw their way into a plastic swimming pool. And here's a possible source for the belief that elephants are afraid of mice: rats are fond of the fatty tissue of the toenails of the great pachyderms.

One of the reasons behind the rat's incessant urge to sample toothpaste tubes, Clorox bottles and shoe leather is the necessity to keep its teeth worn down. As with most of the rodents and the rabbits, the rat possesses a constantly growing set of incisors. If these teeth are not honed to size, the animal will starve. A rat that has lost an upper incisor, say, has nothing against which its corresponding lower tooth can wear itself away; in a few weeks the unopposed tooth will get so long that the rat cannot shut its mouth. If it manages to survive, its life will be terminated when the maverick tooth grows up in a semicircle and penetrates its brain. All told, a rat's incisors may grow more than six inches during his three years of life.

If you are in doubt about this creature's ability to adjust to new conditions, try setting a trap. The intended victim seems to recognize it at once. Sometimes it even pushes the offending object around almost as if to make it snap. Then, after the trap has sprung, the victorious rodent consumes the bait.

A farmer I know even baits his traps with poisoned food; he figures he'll outfox the foxy rats. It works, too. "Why, I've been fooling the rats this way for years," he tells me. But the very fact that he gets a continuous supply of rats proves he never fools *all* of them.

Even professional ratcatchers, from the Pied Piper of Hamelin to the modern exterminator with his impressive apparatus, can seldom get every rat. A few are almost always left. If by chance the rodents are wiped out entirely, a few soon move in from next door. A well-fed female can produce in a year eight to ten litters of eight or ten youngsters each. Each of her offspring is ready to breed on its own in about four months, so the lucky householder is soon right back where he started.

Brother Rat makes his way right along with us wherever we go. He moved West with the pioneers. He went underground into the sewers and subways. There are rats living in the maze of railroad tracks beneath New York City who are born, raise their families and die without ever seeing the light of day.

These rodents have added much to our language. It's the rat that deserts the sinking ship; therefore he is a coward, though it would make no sense for him to remain. If you "rat" on somebody you betray him. Fight like a cornered rat, and you fight to the end—

behavior that's fine in people but wrong in rats. Call a person a rat and you've said everything in that three-letter word, even if neither of you has ever known a single rat personally.

Whether we like it or not, the rat is a perfect adjunct to our activities. Sheltered from all harm, constantly supplied with garbage and packaged products free for the nibbling, kept warm in winter and cool in summer, he fares as well as many a pampered pet. Probably he gets along even better, for he can choose his own food.

The presence of the rat, reminding us of our own slovenly ways, is a constant source of embarrassment. He's one problem you cannot sweep under the rug. Since we've built him a refuge from hawks and owls, and since we take great pains to eliminate every skunk, fox and weasel before it can catch a single rat, we have only ourselves to blame. Like it or not, we've made the rat what he is today.

Our attempts to put our little fellow-traveler in his place have often taken the form of going after the symptoms rather than treating the cause. Instead of buckling down and cleaning up conditions that favor the rat, we've tried to get other creatures to carry out our campaigns for us. I remember once seeing a ferret released under a barn in Connecticut. There was a general alarm among the rats—squealing and chattering and the thumping of bodies frantically trying to escape. A few seconds after the ferret invaded their quarters, rats erupted from all over the barn and fled into the grass. But even the nimble ferret couldn't catch them all. Doubtless the remaining rats were back in a short time.

The rats in Hawaii got to be such a nuisance that the swift little mongoose was imported from Asia to deal with them. We saw the results when we visited the Islands recently: half a hundred species of ground-nesting birds exterminated completely, chickens and small wild animals in mortal danger of their lives, and mongooses all over the place.

The rats? Doing fine, thanks. It seems that the mongoose runs around largely by day, while the rat is abroad at night. So the paths of these two mammals seldom cross.

While rats make us uncomfortable by reminding us of our own failings, other animals don't seem to be human enough to suit us. We are seldom content to let a dog be a dog, say, and bark and howl and do his doggy best at the fireplug. We take him out on a leash and studiously look the other way. We deodorize skunks and pull the claws out of cats. When I had a pet porcupine a few years ago, a well-meaning friend suggested I de-quill Piney–remove all thirty thousand of his stickers. And she was quite taken aback when she learned I'd had him a whole year and hadn't taught him a single trick.

People seem to have a compulsion to make animals into human beings. We train bears to ride bicycles and teach elephants to stand on their heads. We do not adjust to them; we make them adjust to us. Yet if adaptability is a measure of intelligence, who is the smart one?

It's in the field of learning–how that the rat comes into its own. Rats can be trained to run surprisingly complex mazes. They can learn to open boxes for the food that's inside. They can be taught to recognize a geometric figure or a letter of the alphabet on sight. These are just laboratory stunts, but they show that man's uninvited guest is gifted with a heaping supply of native intelligence.

It also has an outsized helping of just plain pluck. It takes a good cat to kill a full-grown rat. I once witnessed the spectacle of an enraged mother rat steadily backing up a Doberman pinscher. The dog had blundered into her nest while a building was being razed. The Doberman, apparently not wanting to submit to the indignity of an abject rout, retreated up a steep mound of debris. As he scrambled backward, he sent pebbles and sawdust rattling down into the face of the sputtering mother.

She backed him right up over the top of the cellar hole. While she performed the feat, a high-priced bulldozer operator, several sidewalk superintendents of unknown salary, and a sometimes-paid writer watched in complete absorption. But lest you impugn the bravery of that Doberman, consider the experience of a friend of mine who cornered a rat in a garage. She jabbed at him with a rake—and he promptly climbed up the handle and chased her out into the driveway.

For such feats, plus the ability to carry out his own population explosion right in the face of everything man can throw at him, you can't help but admire Rattus. In a very real sense, he is what we have made him, every step of the way. Whether he's in his space suit, his lab coat or his bandit's cloak, you've got to hand it to him.

And hand it to him you'd better. Chances are he'll take it anyway.

An Introduction to Dogs

The dog is man's best friend.
He has a tail on one end.
Up in front he has teeth.
And four legs underneath.

Dogs like to bark.
They like it best after dark.
They not only frighten prowlers away
But also hold the sandman at bay.

A dog that is indoors
To be let out implores.
You let him out and what then?
He wants back in again.

Dogs display reluctance and wrath
If you try to give them a bath.
They bury bones in hideaways
And half the time they trot sideaways.

They cheer up people who are frowning,
And rescue people who are drowning.
They also track mud on beds,
And chew people's clothes to shreds.

Dogs in the country have fun.
They run and run and run.
But in the city this species
Is dragged around on leashes.

Dogs are upright as a steeple
And much more loyal than people.
Well people may be reprehensibler
But that's probably because they are sensibler.

Ogden Nash

Catalog

Cats sleep fat and walk thin.
Cats, when they sleep, slump;
When they wake, they pull in—
And where the plump's been
There's skin.
Cats walk thin.

Cats wait in a lump,
Jump in a streak.
Cats, when they jump, are sleek
As a grape slipping its skin—
They have technique.
Oh, cats don't creak.
They sneak.

Cats sleep fat.
They spread comfort beneath them
Like a good mat,
As if they picked the place
And then sat.
You walk around one
As if he were the City Hall
After that.

If male,
A cat is apt to sing on a major scale;
This concert is for everybody, this
Is wholesale.
For a baton, he wields his tail.

(He is also found,
When happy, to resound
With an enclosed private sound.)

Rosalie Moore

l(a)

Cummings tries to make not only word and line arrangements work for him but syllables, letters, numbers, and punctuation. This poem is a puzzle—a word scramble that has in it an idea waiting to be shared with any reader who's a good detective.

l(a

le
af
fa

ll

s)
one
l

iness

e.e. cummings

Some clues:

What letter that appears often in the poem is both a letter and a number on a typewriter?

Do any of the letter combinations make sense by themselves? Try combining until you see a whole.

Dandelions

You won't find them in places where society goes,
Like flower shows.
Their affections
Run more to junk yards and other low-rent sections—
Not flowers to make perfume of or wear.
People see them in their lawns and swear.
Cows eat them and their milk tastes funny.
Bees make them into honey.
The farmer turns them under with his plow,
Or makes them into wine if he knows how.
They hang around street corners on pipestem legs,
And taste good in salad with vinegar and hard-boiled
eggs.
In broken bricks and cinders they
Do well. Also in clay.
Hills they prefer to valleys.
They like to grow
Where kids go,

In vacant lots and alleys.
Little girls use them for various things,
Such as money. They put them on strings,
Or hold them under their chins to see if they like butter.
Golfers knock their heads off with a putter.
You can split them with your tongue to make long
curls,
Which small comedians wear to look like girls.
They hug the earth where lawnmowers mow,
And so survive.
Elsewhere they stretch taller.

In areas where nothing else will grow
They thrive—
More like the sun than sunflowers,
Only smaller.
They can't be stopped although you hoe and spray
them;
The best that you can hope is to delay them.
No skirmish ever proves to be the last;
No victory quite manages to stay won.
They seem to propagate about as fast
As a middle-aged gardener can run.
There isn't any more that you can say
About these tawny, undesired plants
(Teeth of the lion is what they're called in France)
Except that certain things are here to stay,
Things that don't pertain to public good,
Such as firecrackers, unplanned parenthood,
Snowballs, or a bedtime story—
Things you'd never dream
Of including in a modern social scheme.
Dandelions fall in this category.

Will Stanton

How does the poet feel about dandelions? Do you respond to them that way? Does your father?

The Sloth

In moving-slow he has no Peer.
You ask him something in his ear;
He thinks about it for a Year;

And, then, before he says a Word
There, upside down (unlike a Bird)
He will assume that you have Heard—

A most Ex-as-per-at-ing Lug.
But should you call his manner Smug,
He'll sigh and give his Branch a Hug;

Then off again to Sleep he goes,
Still swaying gently by his Toes,
And you just *know* he knows he knows.

Theodore Roethke

Poets sometimes force us to read words a little differently from how we normally read them. Why do you suppose "Exasperating" is written the way it is? And why is "know" italicized in the last line?

The Eagle

He clasps the crag with crooked hands;
Close to the sun in lonely lands,
Ring'd with the azure world, he stands.

The wrinkled sea beneath him crawls;
He watches from his mountain walls,
And like a thunderbolt he falls.

Alfred, Lord Tennyson

Explosion

Something in the wild cherry–
the cat or another caution–
triggers the starlings and the tree
explodes. Who would have thought
so many pieces of life in one tree?
The air shakes with their whirligig.
The first have already lit across the field
before the last one's out.

They fling their bridge of lives
and of some sort of reason
across the field, a black
rainbow over my surprise. . . .

John Ciardi

Can you think of any other "explosions" you have seen in nature?

A Bird Came Down the Walk

A bird came down the walk–
He did not know I saw–
He bit an angle-worm in halves
And ate the fellow, raw.

And then he drank a dew
From a convenient grass,
And then hopped sidewise to the wall
To let a beetle pass.

He glanced with rapid eyes
That hurried all abroad,–
They looked like frightened beads, I thought–
He stirred his velvet head

Like one in danger; cautious,
I offered him a crumb,
And he unrolled his feathers
And rowed him softer home

Than oars divide the ocean,
Too silver for a seam–
Or butterflies, off banks of noon,
Leap, plashless, as they swim.

Emily Dickinson

Is it the kind of bird that makes the difference in the last three poems or what the poet selects to tell us? Which one do you like the best?

Warning: This man is not
dangerous, answers to any name
Responds to love, don't
call him or he will come.
"Unwanted"

The Whistle Blows

Ernie Pyle

During World War II many newspapermen accompanied our armed forces on the battlefields of Europe, Africa, and the South Pacific. It was their job to send home firsthand reports of the fighting and of the war's progress. One of these newsmen especially endeared himself to Americans by his sympathetic and sensitive stories about the ordinary GI, or foot soldier. This reporter was Ernie Pyle. So well and interestingly written were his newspaper columns that in 1944 Pyle's war reporting won him the coveted Pulitzer prize. Two years later he was killed when landing with our American soldiers on a South Pacific island near Okinawa.

In this selection from *Brave Men,* a book of Pyle's collected writings, he tells of the greatest land and sea operation in history—the Allied invasion of France which took place on June 6, 1944. For many months before this invasion, newspapers and bulletins had spoken of the coming event as D-Day (the name given to the date of a planned military operation). But no one knew what day the invasion would actually take place, or just where it would occur. Ernie Pyle's account of the Allied landing on the Normandy beachhead conveys to us in poignantly human terms the drama of that great military epic.

All of us had dreaded the trip, for we had expected attacks from U-boats, E-boats, and at nighttime, from aircraft. Yet nothing whatever happened.

We were at sea for a much longer time than it would ordinarily take to make a bee-line journey from England to France. As we came down, the English Channel was crammed with forces going both ways. Minesweepers had swept wide channels for us all the way. Each channel was miles wide and marked with buoys.

Surely we saw there before us more ships than any human being had ever seen before at one glance. And going north were other vast convoys, some composed of fast liners speeding back to England for new loads of troops and equipment.

As far as you could see in every direction the ocean was infested with ships. There must have been every type of ocean-going vessel in the world. I even thought I saw a paddlewheel steamer in the distance, but that was probably an illusion.

There were battleships and all other kinds of warships clear down to patrol boats. There were great fleets of Liberty ships. There were fleets of luxury liners turned into troop transports, and fleets of big landing craft and tank carriers and tankers. And in and out through it all were nondescript ships—converted yachts, river boats, tugs, and barges.

The best way I can describe that vast armada and the frantic urgency of the traffic is to suggest that you visualize New York Harbor on its busiest day of the year and then just enlarge that scene until it takes in all the ocean the human eye can reach, clear around the horizon. And over the horizon, imagine dozens of times that number of vessels.

Everything was magnificently organized, and every ship, even the tiniest one, was always under exact orders timed to the minute. But at one time our convoy was so pushed along by the wind and the currents that we were five hours ahead of schedule, despite the fact that our engines had been stopped half the time. We adjusted that by circling.

Although we arrived just on time, they weren't ready for us on the beaches, and we spent several hours weaving in and out among the multitude of ships just off the beachhead. Finally we just settled down to await our turn.

That was when the most incongruous—to us—part of the invasion came. There we were in a front-row seat at a great military epic. Shells from battleships were whamming over our heads, and occasionally a dead man floated face downward past us. Hundreds and hundreds of ships laden with death milled around us. We could stand at the rail and see both our shells and German shells exploding on the beaches where struggling men were leaping ashore, desperately hauling guns and equipment through the water.

We were in the very vortex of the war, and yet, as we sat there waiting, two of the men played gin rummy in the wardroom, and Bing Crosby sang "Sweet Leilani" over the ship's phonograph.

Angry shells hitting near us would make heavy thuds as the concussion carried through the water and struck the hull of our ship. But in our wardroom men in gas-impregnated uniforms and wearing life belts sat reading *Life* and listening to the BBC telling us how the war before us was going.

But it wasn't like that ashore. No, it wasn't like that ashore.

Owing to a last-minute alteration in the arrangements, I didn't arrive on the beachhead until the morning after D-day, after our first wave of assault troops had hit the shore.

By the time we got there the beaches had been taken, and the fighting had moved a couple of miles inland. All that remained on the beach were some sniping and artillery fire and the occasional startling blast of a mine geysering brown sand into the air. That plus a gigantic and pitiful litter of wreckage along miles of shore line.

Submerged tanks and overturned boats and burned trucks and shell-shattered jeeps and sad little personal belongings were strewn all over those bitter sands. That plus the bodies of soldiers lying in rows covered with blankets, the toes of their shoes sticking up in a line as though on drill. And other bodies, uncollected, still sprawling grotesquely in the sand or half-hidden by the high grass beyond the beach. That plus an intense, grim determination of work-weary men to get that chaotic beach organized and get all the vital supplies and the reinforcements moving more rapidly over it from the stacked-up ships standing in droves out at sea.

After it was over it seemed to me a pure miracle that we ever took the beach at all. For some of our units it was easy, but in the special sector where I landed, our troops faced such odds that our getting ashore was like my whipping Joe Louis down to a pulp. The men who did it on that beach were men of the First and Twenty-ninth divisions.

I want to tell you what the opening of the second front in that one sector entailed, so that you can know and appreciate and forever be humbly grateful to those both dead and alive who did it for you.

Ashore, facing us, were more enemy troops than we had in our assault waves. The advantages were all theirs, the disadvantages all ours. The Germans were dug into positions they had been working on for months, although they were not entirely complete. A 100-foot bluff a couple of hundred yards back from the beach had great concrete gun emplacements built right into the hilltop. These opened to the sides instead of to the front, thus making it hard for naval fire from the sea to reach them. They could shoot parallel with the shore and cover every foot of it for miles with artillery fire.

Then they had hidden machine-gun nests on the forward slopes with crossfire taking in every inch of the beach. These nests were connected by networks of trenches, so that the German gunners could move about without exposing themselves.

Throughout the length of the beach, running zigzag a couple of hundred yards back from the shore line, was an immense V-shaped ditch fifteen feet deep. Nothing could cross it, not even men on foot, until fills had been made. And in other places at the far end of the beach, where the ground was flatter, they had great concrete walls. These were blasted by our naval gunfire or by explosives set by hand after we got ashore.

Our only exits from the beach were several swales or valleys, each about a hundred yards wide. The Germans made the most of these funnel-like traps, sowing them with buried mines. They also contained barbed-wire entanglement with mines attached, hidden ditches, and machine guns firing from the slopes.

All this was on the shore. But our men had to go through a maze nearly as deadly before they even got ashore. Underwater obstacles were terrific. Under the water the Germans had whole fields of evil devices to catch our boats. Several days after the landing we had cleared only channels through them and still could not approach the length of the beach with our ships. Even then some ship or boat would hit one of those mines and be knocked out of commission.

The Germans had masses of great six-pronged spiders—made of railroad iron and standing shoulder-high—just beneath the surface of the water, for our landing craft to run into. They had huge logs buried in the sand, pointing upward and outward, their tops just below the water. Attached to the logs were mines.

In addition to these obstacles they had floating mines offshore, land mines buried in the sand of the beach, and more mines in checkerboard rows in the tall grass beyond the sand. And the enemy had four men on shore for every three men we had approaching the shore.

And yet we got on.

Beach landings are always planned to a schedule that is set far ahead of time. They all have to be timed for everything to mesh and for the following waves of troops to be standing off the beach and ready to land at the right moment. Some elements of the assault force are to break through quickly, push on inland, and attack the most obvious enemy strong points. It is usually the plan for units to be inland, attacking gun positions from behind, within a matter of minutes after the first men hit the beach.

I have always been amazed at the speed called for in these plans. Schedules will call for engineers to land at H-hour plus 2 minutes, and service troops at H-hour plus 30 minutes, and even for press censors to land at H-hour plus 75 minutes. But in the attack on my special portion of the beach—the toughest spot of all—the schedule didn't hold.

Our men simply could not get past the beach. They were pinned down right on the water's edge by an inhuman wall of fire from the bluff. Our first waves were on that beach for hours, instead of a few minutes, before they could begin working inland.

The foxholes were still there—dug at the very edge of the water, in the sand and the small jumbled rocks that formed parts of the beach.

Medical corpsmen attended the wounded as best they could. Men were killed as they stepped out of landing craft. An officer whom I knew got a bullet through the head just as the door of his landing craft was let down. Some men were drowned.

The first crack in the beach defenses was finally accomplished by terrific and wonderful naval gunfire, which knocked out the big emplacements. Epic stories have been told of destroyers that ran right up into shallow water and had it out point-blank with the big guns in those concrete emplacements ashore.

When the heavy fire stopped, our men were organized by their officers and pushed on inland, circling machine-gun nests and taking them from the rear.

As one officer said, the only way to take a beach is to face it and keep going. It is costly at first, but it's the only way. If the men are pinned down on the beach, dug in and out of action, they might as well not be there at all. They hold up the waves behind them, and nothing is gained.

Our men were pinned down for a while, but finally they stood up and went through, and so we took that beach and accomplished our landing. In the light of a couple of days of retrospection, we sat and talked and called it a miracle that our men ever got on at all or were able to stay on.

They suffered casualties. And yet considering the entire beachhead assault, including other units that had a much easier time, our total casualties in driving that wedge into the continent of Europe were remarkably low—only a fraction of what our commanders had been prepared to accept.

And those units that were so battered and went through such horror pushed on inland without rest, their spirits high, their egotism in victory almost reaching the smart-alecky stage.

Their tails were up. "We've done it again," they said. They figured that the rest of the Army wasn't needed at all. Which proves that, while their judgment in this respect was bad, they certainly had the spirit that wins battles and, eventually, wars.

When I went ashore on the soil of France, the first

thing I wanted to do was hunt up the other correspondents I had said good-by to a few days previously in England, and see how they had fared. Before the day of invasion we had accepted it as a fact that not everybody would come through alive.

Correspondents sort of gang together. They know the ins and outs of wars, and they all work at it in much the same manner. So I knew about where to look, and I didn't have much trouble finding them.

It was early in the morning, before the boys had started out on their day's round of covering the war. I found them in foxholes dug into the rear slope of a grassy hill about a half mile from the beach. I picked them out from a distance, because I could spot Jack Thompson's beard. He was sitting on the edge of a foxhole lacing his paratrooper boots. About a dozen correspondents were there, among them three especially good friends of mine—Thompson, Don Whitehead, and Tex O'Reilly.

First of all we checked with each other on what we had heard about other correspondents. Most of them were O.K. One had been killed, and one was supposed to have been lost on a sunken ship, but we didn't know who. One or two had been wounded. Three of our best friends had not been heard from at all, and it looked bad. They subsequently turned up safe.

The boys were unshaved and their eyes were red. Their muscles were stiff and their bodies ached. They had carried ashore only their typewriters and some K rations. They had gone two days without sleep and then had slept on the ground without blankets, in wet clothes.

But none of that mattered too much after what they had been through. They were in a sort of daze from the exhaustion and mental turmoil of battle. When anyone asked a question, it would take them a few seconds to focus their thoughts and give an answer.

Two of them in particular had been through all the frightful nightmare that the assault troops had experienced, because they had gone ashore with them.

Don Whitehead hit the beach with one regiment just an hour after H-hour, Thompson at the same time with another regiment. They were on the beaches for more than four hours under that hideous cloudburst of shells and bullets.

Jack Thompson said, "You've never seen a beach like it before. Dead and wounded men were lying so thick you could hardly take a step. One officer was killed only two feet away from me."

Whitehead was still asleep when I went to his foxhole. I said, "Get up, you lazy so-and-so." He started grinning without even opening his eyes, for he knew who it was.

It was hard for him to wake up. He had been unable to sleep, from sheer exhaustion, and had taken a sleeping tablet.

Don had managed to steal one blanket on the beach and had that wrapped around him. He had taken off his shoes. His feet were so sore from walking in wet shoes and socks that he had to give them some air.

Finally he began to get himself up. "I don't know why I'm alive at all," he said. "It was really awful. For hours there on the beach the shells were so close they were throwing mud and rocks all over you. It was so bad after a while you didn't care whether you got hit or not."

Don fished in a cardboard ration box for some cigarettes. He pulled out an envelope and threw it into the bushes. "They aren't worth a thing," he said. The envelope contained antiseasickness tablets.

"I was sick as could be while we were circling around

in our landing craft waiting to come ashore," he said. "Everybody was sick. Soldiers were on the floor of the LCVP, sick as dogs."

Tex O'Reilly rode around in a boat for six hours waiting to get ashore. Everybody was wet and cold and seasick and scared. War is so romantic—if you're far away from it. Whitehead had probably been in more amphibious landings than any other correspondent over there. I know of six he made, four of them murderously tough. And he said, "I think I have gone on one too many of these things. Not because of what might happen to me personally, but I've lost my perspective. It's like dreaming the same nightmare over and over again, and when you try to write, you feel that you have written it all before. You can't think of any new or different words to say it with."

I knew only too well what he meant.

It is an ironic thing about correspondents who go in on the first few days of an invasion story. They are the only correspondents capable of telling the full and intimate drama and horror of the thing. And yet they are the ones who can't get their copy out to the world. By the time they do, events have swirled on, and the world doesn't care any more.

There that morning in their foxholes on the slope of the hill, those correspondents were mainly worried about the communications situation. Although they had landed with the first wave, they felt sure that none of their copy had ever reached America. And even I, a day behind them, felt no assurance that my feeble reports would ever see the light of day. But in philosophical moments I can think of greater catastrophes than that.

I took a walk along the historic coast of Normandy in the country of France. It was a lovely day for strolling along the seashore. Men were sleeping on the sand, some of them forever. Men were floating in the water, but they didn't know they were in the water, for they were dead.

I walked for a mile and a half along the water's edge of our many-miled invasion beach. I walked slowly, for the detail on that beach was infinite.

The wreckage was vast and startling. The awful waste and destruction of war, even aside from the loss of human life, has always been one of its outstanding features to those who are in it. Anything and everything is expendable. And we did expend on our beachhead in Normandy during those first few hours.

For a mile out from the beach there were scores of tanks and trucks and boats that were not visible, for they were at the bottom of the water—swamped by overloading, or hit by shell, or sunk by mines. Most of their crews were lost.

There were trucks tipped half over and swamped, partly sunken barges, and the angled-up corners of jeeps, and small landing craft half submerged. And at low tide you could still see those vicious six-pronged iron snares that helped snag and wreck them.

On the beach itself, high and dry, were all kinds of wrecked vehicles. There were tanks that had only just made the beach before being knocked out. There were jeeps that had burned to a dull gray. There were big derricks on caterpillar treads that didn't quite make it. There were half-tracks carrying office equipment that had been made into a shambles by a single shell hit, their interiors still holding the useless equipage of smashed typewriters, telephones, office files.

There were LCTs turned completely upside down and lying on their backs, and how they got that way I don't know. There were boats stacked on top of each other, their sides caved in, their suspension doors knocked off.

In this shore-line museum of carnage there were abandoned rolls of barbed wire and smashed bulldozers and stacks of discarded life belts and piles of shells still waiting to be moved. In the water floated empty life rafts and soldiers' packs and ration boxes, and mysterious oranges. On the beach lay snarled rolls of telephone wire and steel matting and stacks of rusting rifles.

On the beach lay, expended, sufficient men and mechanism for a small war. They were gone forever now. And yet we could afford it.

We could afford it because we were on, we had our toe hold, and behind us there were such enormous replacements for this wreckage on the beach that you could hardly conceive of the sum total. Men and equipment were flowing from England in such a gigantic stream that it made the waste on the beachhead seem like nothing at all, really nothing at all.

But there was another and more human litter. It extended in a thin little line, just like a high-water mark, for miles along the beach. This was the strewn personal gear, gear that would never be needed again by those who fought and died to give us our entrance into Europe.

There in a jumbled row for mile on mile were soldiers' packs. There were socks and shoe polish, sewing kits, diaries, Bibles, hand grenades. There were the latest letters from home, with the address on each one neatly razored out—one of the security precautions enforced before the boys embarked.

There were toothbrushes and razors, and snapshots of families back home staring up at you from the sand.

There were pocketbooks, metal mirrors, extra trousers, and bloody, abandoned shoes. There were broken-handled shovels and portable radios, smashed almost beyond recognition, and mine detectors, twisted and ruined.

There were torn pistol belts and canvas water buckets, first-aid kits, and jumbled heaps of life belts. I picked up a pocket Bible with a soldier's name in it and put it in my jacket. I carried it half a mile or so and then put it back down on the beach. I don't know why I picked it up or why I put it down again.

Soldiers carry strange things ashore with them. In every invasion there is at least one soldier hitting the beach at H-hour with a banjo slung over his shoulder. The most ironic piece of equipment marking our beach—this beach first of despair, then of victory—was a tennis racket that a soldier had brought along. It lay lonesomely on the sand, clamped in its press, not a string broken.

Two of the most dominant items in the beach refuse were cigarettes and writing paper. Each soldier was issued a carton of cigarettes just before he started. That day those cartons by the thousand, water-soaked and spilled out, marked the line of our first savage blow.

Writing paper and air-mail envelopes came second. The boys had intended to do a lot of writing in France. The letters—now forever incapable of being written—that might have filled those blank abandoned pages!

Always there are dogs in every invasion. There was a dog still on the beach, still pitifully looking for his masters.

He stayed at the water's edge, near a boat that lay twisted and half sunk at the waterline. He barked appealingly to every soldier who approached, trotted eagerly along with him for a few feet, and then, sensing himself unwanted in all the haste, he would run back to wait in vain for his own people at his own empty boat.

Over and around this long, thin line of personal anguish, fresh men were rushing vast supplies to keep our armies pushing on into France. Other squads of men picked amidst the wreckage to salvage ammunition and equipment that was still usable.

Men worked and slept on the beach for days before the last D-day victim was taken away for burial.

I stepped over the form of one youngster whom I thought dead. But when I looked down I saw he was only sleeping. He was very young and very tired. He lay on one elbow, his hand suspended in the air about six inches from the ground. And in the palm of his hand he held a large, smooth rock.

I stood and looked at him a long time. He seemed in his sleep to hold that rock lovingly, as though it were his last link with a vanishing world. I have no idea at all why he went to sleep with the rock in his hand, or what kept him from dropping it once he was asleep. It was just one of those little things without explanation that a person remembers for a long time.

The strong, swirling tides of the Normandy coast line shifted the contours of the sandy beach as they moved in and out. They carried soldiers' bodies out to sea, and later they returned them. They covered the corpses of heroes with sand, and then in their whims they uncovered them.

As I plowed out over the wet sand, I walked around what seemed to be a couple of pieces of driftwood sticking out of the sand. But they weren't driftwood. They were a soldier's two feet. He was completely covered except for his feet; the toes of his GI shoes pointed toward the land he had come so far to see, and which he saw so briefly.

A few hundred yards back on the beach was a high bluff. Up there we had a tent hospital, and a barbed wire enclosure for prisoners of war. From up there you could see far up and down the beach, in a spectacular crow's-nest view, and far out to sea.

And standing out there on the water beyond all this wreckage was the greatest armada man has ever seen. You simply could not believe the gigantic collection of ships that lay out there waiting to unload. Looking from the bluff, it lay thick and clear to the far horizon of the sea and on beyond, and it spread out to the sides and was miles wide.

As I stood up there I noticed a group of freshly taken German prisoners standing by. They had not yet been put in the prison cage. They were just standing there, a couple of doughboys guarding them with tommy guns.

The prisoners too were looking out to sea—the same bit of sea that for months and years had been so safely empty before their gaze. Now they stood staring almost as if in a trance. They didn't say a word to each other. They didn't need to. The expression on their faces was something forever unforgettable. In it was the final, horrified acceptance of their doom.

A newspaper reporter and a poet both try to observe carefully and vividly present those observations to their readers. What impressed you most about Pyle's essay?

Now read "Disabled." Which writer makes the most vivid impression on you?

Disabled

He sat in a wheeled chair, waiting for dark,
And shivered in his ghastly suit of grey,
Legless, sewn short at elbow. Through the park
Voices of boys rang saddening like a hymn,
Voices of play and pleasure after day,
Till gathering sleep had mothered them from him.

* * *

About this time Town used to swing so gay
When glow-lamps budded in the light blue trees,
And girls glanced lovelier as the air grew dim,—
In the old times, before he threw away his knees.
Now he will never feel again how slim
Girls' waists are, or how warm their subtle hands;
All of them touch him like some queer disease.

* * *

There was an artist silly for his face,
For it was younger than his youth, last year.
Now, he is old; his back will never brace;
He's lost his colour very far from here,
Poured it down shell-holes till the veins ran dry,
And half his lifetime lapsed in the hot race,
And leap of purple spurted from his thigh.

* * *

One time he liked a blood-smear down his leg,
After the matches, carried shoulder-high.
It was after football, when he'd drunk a peg,
He thought he'd better join.—He wonders why.
Someone had said he'd look a god in kilts,
That's why; and may be, too, to please his Meg;
Aye, that was it, to please the giddy jilts
He asked to join. He didn't have to beg;
Smiling they wrote his lie; aged nineteen years.

Germans he scarcely thought of; all their guilt,
And Austria's, did not move him. And no fears
Of Fear came yet. He thought of jewelled hilts
For daggers in plaid socks; of smart salutes;
And care of arms; and leave; and pay arrears;
Esprit de corps; and hints for young recruits.
And soon, he was drafted out with drums and cheers.

* * *

Some cheered him home, but not as crowds cheer Goal.
Only a solemn man who brought him fruits
Thanked him; and then inquired about his soul.

* * *

Now, he will spend a few sick years in Institutes,
And do what things the rules consider wise,
And take whatever pity they may dole.
To-night he noticed how the women's eyes
Passed from him to the strong men that were whole.
How cold and late it is! Why don't they come
And put him into bed? Why don't they come?

Wilfred Owen

The Battle of the Ants

Henry David Thoreau

Think how surprised Thoreau's neighbors must have been when he announced his intention to cut himself off from the comforts and distractions of civilization for a while and live alone in the woods. Thoreau thought that men were too much absorbed with "things," and that he could live a simple and more natural life close to nature. So in 1845 he took his ax, his flute, some books, and a spyglass and set off for Walden Pond, near Concord, Massachusetts. Here he built himself a hut on a pine slope, planted potatoes, beans, and corn, and settled down to study nature and observe the creatures of the wild. He had plenty of time also to read and study.

In this manner Thoreau lived for two years and two months on only eight dollars a year, maintaining himself by cultivating his garden and by doing odd jobs, such as boat building. During all this time, as was his custom, he kept a diary, a journal, of his experiences. Some years later he used this diary as material for a book named *Walden, or Life in the Woods.* It is from this book that "The Battle of the Ants" is taken.

One day when I went out to my wood pile, or rather my pile of stumps, I observed two large ants, the one red, the other much larger, nearly half an inch long, and black, fiercely contending with one another. Having once got hold, they never let go, but struggled and wrestled and rolled on the chips incessantly. Looking farther, I was surprised to find that the chips were covered with such combatants—that it was not a *duellum* but a *bellum,* a war between two races of ants, the red always pitted against the black, and frequently two red ones to one black. The legions of those Myrmidons covered all the hills and vales in my woodyard, and the ground was already strewn with the dead and dying, both red and black. It was the only battlefield which I have ever witnessed, the only battlefield I ever trod while the battle was raging; internecine war; the red republicans on the one hand and the black imperialists on the other. On every side they were engaged in deadly combat, yet without any noise that I could hear, and human soldiers never fought so resolutely. I watched a couple that were fast locked in each other's embraces, in a little sunny valley amid the chips, now at noonday prepared to fight till the sun went down or life went out. The smaller red champion had fastened himself like a vise to his adversary's front, and through all the tumblings on that field never for an instant ceased to gnaw at one of his feelers near the root, having already caused the other to go by the board, while the stronger black one dashed him from side to side, and, as I saw on looking nearer, had already divested him of several of his members. They fought with more pertinacity than bulldogs. Neither manifested the least disposition to retreat. It was evident that their battle cry was "Conquer or die."

In the meanwhile there came along a single red ant on the hillside of this valley, evidently full of excitement, who either had dispatched his foe or had not yet taken part in the battle (probably the latter, for he had lost none of his limbs), whose mother had charged him to return with his shield or upon it. Or perchance he was some Achilles, who had nourished his wrath apart, and had now come to avenge or rescue his Patroclus. He saw this unequal combat from afar—for the blacks were nearly twice the size of the red; he drew near with rapid pace till he stood on his guard within half an inch of the combatants; then, watching his opportunity, he sprang upon the black warrior and commenced his operations near the root of his right foreleg, leaving the foe to select among his own members; and so there were three united for life, as if a new kind of attraction had been invented which put all other locks and cements to shame.

I should not have wondered by this time to find that they had their respective musical bands stationed on some eminent chip, and playing their national airs the while, to excite the slow and cheer the dying combatants. I was myself excited somewhat even as if they had been men. The more you think of it, the less the difference. And certainly there is not a fight recorded in Concord history, at least, if in the history of America, that will bear a moment's comparison with this, whether for the numbers engaged in it, or for the patriotism and heroism displayed. For numbers and for carnage it was an Austerlitz. I have no doubt that it was a principle these ant armies fought for, as much as our ancestors, and not to avoid a threepenny tax on their tea; and the results of this battle will be as important and memorable to those whom it concerns as those of the battle of Bunker Hill, at least.

I took up the chip on which the three I have particularly described were struggling, carried it into my house, and placed it under a tumbler on my window sill, in order to see the issue. Holding a microscope to the first-mentioned red ant, I saw that, though he was assiduously gnawing at the near foreleg of his enemy,

having severed his remaining feeler, his own breast was all torn away, exposing what vitals he had there to the jaws of the black warrior, whose breastplate was apparently too thick for him to pierce; and the dark carbuncles of the sufferer's eyes shone with ferocity such as war only could excite. They struggled half an hour longer under the tumbler, and when I looked again the black soldier had severed the heads of his foes from their bodies, and the still-living heads were hanging on either side of him like ghastly trophies at his saddle-bow, still apparently as firmly fastened as ever, and he was endeavoring with feeble struggles, being without feelers and with only the remnant of a leg, and I know not how many other wounds, to divest himself of them; which at length, after half an hour more, he accomplished. I raised the glass, and he went off over the window sill in that crippled state. Whether he finally survived that combat, and spent the remainder of his days in some Hôtel des Invalides, I do not know, but I thought that his industry would not be worth much thereafter. I never learned which party was victorious, nor the cause of the war, but I felt for the rest of the day as if I had my feelings excited and harrowed by witnessing the struggle, the ferocity and carnage, of a human battle before my door.

Can you see any reason for this essay following "Disabled"? Which of the two could you more easily forget? Why?

Peril from the Sky

from Senior Scholastic *magazine*

Take a deep breath. Feel the cool air pushing up your nostrils and filling your lungs. Air—clean, fresh, invisible, inexhaustible.

If you live in a large American city, you have just inhaled about seventy thousand particles of dust, plus a varying mixture of harmful gases. That's a startling fact. Here are a few more:

Chicago loses forty percent of its natural sunlight to air pollution.

Pollution—not insects or weather—poses the largest threat to New Jersey farms.

Fumes from a phosphate plant have softened the bones of cattle in Polk County, Florida.

The death rate in New York City rose ten percent during a period of heavy air pollution in 1966.

People across the country and around the world are learning that the air they breathe—the air they have always taken for granted—is neither clean nor fresh nor invisible nor, as some of the more pessimistic scientists predict, inexhaustible.

Man can purify water before he drinks it, but unless he wears a gas mask, he must breathe the air as it comes. Every year it comes to man with an increasing load of airborne garbage, the product of his own cleverness and indifference. Last year Americans tossed a whopping 143 million tons of pollutants into the skies.

Besides spreading a blanket of gloom over much of the country, pollutants are destructive. The United States Department of Health, Education and Welfare (HEW) estimates that the ravages of air pollution cost every man, woman, and child in the United States about

$65 a year. In heavily polluted cities the average is closer to $200.

Air pollution cracks the paint on houses, eats away at stone, tarnishes copper and silver, rusts iron, causes runs in nylon stockings, and cracks rubber tires. Houses and clothes must be cleaned more frequently.

Nor are people outside the city safe from the ravages of pollution. Winds can carry pollution to farmlands one hundred miles away from the nearest factory.

Many plants are even more sensitive to polluted air than human beings are. In California, for example, orchid growers have had to move away from heavily polluted areas. Airborne gases have stunted the growth of citrus trees in Florida. A Presidential Science Advisory Committee said that crop damage caused by air pollution amounts to $500 million a year in the United States.

But more important, and impossible to calculate in dollars, are the dangers to human health. The United Nations World Health Organization has identified more than one hundred different pollutants, but it is difficult for doctors and scientists to pinpoint them in the air we breathe. They do know that people living in heavily polluted areas suffer from more respiratory diseases than people who live elsewhere: more colds, more bronchitis, more emphysema, asthma, and pneumonia. Breathing normally in a heavily polluted city is equal to smoking a pack or more of cigarettes a day.

Winds from an industrial complex in New Jersey blow across the northern half of Staten Island, New York. The southern half of the island has cleaner air. Twice as many women die of respiratory cancer in the northern part of Staten Island.

The day-to-day effect of dirty air is hard to measure, and most people take it for granted. Stinging eyes, a

runny nose . . . Usually it takes a disaster to make people aware of the dangers of air pollution. And there have been several:

In 1930 a thick, stagnant fog spread over the Meuse Valley of Belgium. By the third day, sixty-three persons were dead and six thousand ill.

The small industrial town of Donora, Pa., was hit by smog in 1948. When the smog lifted, twenty people had died and half the town's population of fourteen thousand had been taken ill.

A killer smog in London took four thousand lives in four days in 1952.

These disasters occurred during a natural phenomenon called a "temperature inversion." Air is generally cooler the farther away it is from the surface of the earth. Warm air near the ground rises, carrying with it smoke and fumes. But occasionally a layer of warm air forms in the upper atmosphere, sealing in the air below and keeping the pollutants near the ground.

Air pollution isn't new. Nature herself polluted the air even before the age of man. Erupting volcanoes, forest fires, and swampland sent smoke and gases into the atmosphere. But nature could take care of her own wastes with rain, winds, and air currents. Then man came along and built fires of his own. Even the ancient Romans complained about city soot on their togas.

Population grew, cities grew, pollution grew. Man began to burn coal instead of wood. By 1661, English scientist John Evelyn wrote that there was "a dismal cloud over London."

In the nineteenth and twentieth centuries, the chemical industry turned out many new products which, says author Lucy Kavaler in her book *Dangerous Air,* "helped raise the standard of living and lower the standard of air."

Man has continued to use air as a dumping place for the wastes of these products of progress. The smokestack and dirty air have become a part of the American landscape.

What are the major pollutants? And where do they all come from?

Air pollution has two major causes: (1) moving automobiles, and (2) stationary sources such as factories, power plants, and oil-burning heating units.

Automobiles account for some sixty percent of all the air pollution in the U.S. Their gasoline-burning engines emit carbon monoxide—a colorless, odorless gas which can cause dizziness, headache, and tiredness, and can kill in sufficient quantities—and hydrocarbons, one of the principal ingredients of smog. There are ninety million cars in the United States and their numbers are growing two and a half times as fast as the population.

Factories, power plants, and heating units burn coal and oil, which give off oxides of sulphur and nitrogen. Sulphur oxides affect the respiratory system and attack such diverse materials as paint and stone. Nitrogen oxides give the sky a brownish haze.

Some efforts have been made to clean up the air. In Los Angeles, for example, industry was forced by the city to clean up almost overnight. Los Angeles industry is now the cleanest in the country, but smog still hangs over the city. Industry, it turned out, accounted for only ten percent of the smog in Los Angeles. Automobiles contributed the other ninety percent.

There are a few success stories in battling air pollution. Industry in the United States spent half a billion dollars last year for controls. The federal government passed the Air Quality Act of 1967, setting up a program of research into the dangers of air pollution and providing federal assistance to states and regions. If the states don't do their job properly, the United States Secretary of Health, Education and Welfare can step in to enforce air quality standards.

Something can be done. Pollutants *can* be trapped before they pour out of smokestacks—and a pollution-free car *can* be built. But federal laws would be needed to bring about a nationwide system of environment control.

As a HEW publication says: "Air pollution is the inevitable consequence of neglect. It can be controlled when that neglect is no longer tolerated. It will be controlled when the people of America, through their elected representatives, demand the right to air that they and their children can breathe without fear."

Does that last paragraph affect you enough to "demand the right to air"? Remember the poem "Smog"? Can you think of another comparison for the problem of pollution after reading this essay?

Rock Bottom

Lorenz Graham

Everybody knew Rock Bottom.

Everybody knew him and almost everybody liked him. They liked him and they laughed at him. He said he liked to see people laughing, and he was always clowning. He wanted to make people laugh, grownups and us kids, too—John Berry and me, and the rest of us.

The first time you saw Rock Bottom you would think he was just a ball of fat. That's when you would laugh. Rock Bottom was fat, but he was big, too. He was big and he was wide and he was strong.

Rock Bottom worked at one of the wrecking yards over by the railroad. The man paid him by the hour. The man said he was paying by the hour, but Rock Bottom didn't get regular pay. He wasn't eighteen years old yet, and he wasn't supposed to be working in a place like that. The man wouldn't give Rock Bottom a man's pay, and nobody else would give Rock Bottom a job.

So Rock Bottom made enough money to help his folks buy groceries and enough to buy burgers and hot dogs and cold drinks for his friends.

He was so strong.

He could pick up most anything. He said that if you could put a handle on it, he could pick up one end of a car—not just one of those VW's or something like that, but a Chevy or a Ford. We believed him, too. The men at the wrecking yard said Rock Bottom didn't know his strength.

He was strong and he was big and he wasn't afraid. Nobody tried to fight with him. Anybody who thought about fighting him would take a good look and they would stop thinking like that.

Like the man on a street-paving job. I saw that myself.

Rock Bottom is coming down the street when this lead man on a paving job is mad at a kid. The man is hollering and cussing and saying what he will do to the kid, like he is going to bust the kid's head if the kid jumps over the place where they are putting down new paving.

The kid is standing on the sidewalk by this time and he is saying he didn't hurt the paving; he didn't touch it—just jumped over it, that's all.

Rock Bottom just stood there and listened. After

while he thought he knew what it was all about and then he said what he had to say. He didn't say it so loud, but the man could sure hear him. I mean Rock Bottom didn't holler. He just said it.

He said, "You ain't going to hit that little boy."

The man stopped hollering. He looked at Rock Bottom.

He said, "What you say?"

Rock Bottom said, "You ain't going to hit no little nine, ten-year-old kid."

The man really got mad then.

He started all over again, but this time it was Rock Bottom he was mad at. He was cussing, saying everything he could think of. He had a job to do and he wasn't going to let anybody stop his work, and it was city work and he would call the police and have anybody locked up who tried to hold up the job.

Then he said, "Who do you think you are, anyway?" meaning Rock Bottom. The paving man never saw Rock Bottom before.

Rock Bottom just stood there and listened, and when the man stopped to get his breath, Rock Bottom started talking back at him.

"It's like I said, man. You ain't going to hit that little kid." Rock Bottom still wasn't talking loud. "And that's what I mean. If you got to hit somebody, let it be somebody your size."

The man started cussing loud. He jumped over to the pile of tools and turned around with a long, heavy stick. It was a pick handle.

He started for Rock Bottom, but Rock Bottom didn't run. He didn't move. He just looked at the lead man and he said, not hollering, but loud enough for everybody to hear him, "Okay, then. Come on!"

And Rock Bottom started cussing, too, calling the

man everything bad and daring him to come and saying if he hit once he better hit hard 'cause it would be the last time he ever would hit anybody.

The man started toward Rock Bottom. Everybody was looking–people passing by and the other men working on the street, the little kid and his friends. Everybody stopped. Rock Bottom stopped talking. Everybody was waiting. The man stood there looking at Rock Bottom, and Rock Bottom stood there looking at the man.

Somebody laughed. It was a woman.

The little kid was standing off a safe distance. He hadn't said anything. Then he said, loud, sounding like a woman, "That man is scared of Rock Bottom. He scared!"

The boy was right and everybody could see it. The man looked around. He saw everybody standing around just waiting, waiting and laughing-like. He was sure mad. You could see it, but he wasn't going up on Rock Bottom.

That's the way Rock Bottom was.

You didn't have to be afraid of him. He didn't jump on nobody. He didn't talk loud. He didn't make like bad. He really didn't know his strength. There wasn't nobody who wanted to try his strength, either.

In the wrecking yard people get hurt. They have a lot of heavy steel. Then there's glass. They break up old cars with crowbars and hammers and cut them up with welding torches, the kind they say you're not supposed to watch because it will make you blind. Sometimes they stack things up real high and the stuff falls over. Lots of people get hurt. They can get killed, too. You're supposed to be eighteen to work in a place like that.

That's why Rock Bottom wasn't supposed to be working in the wrecking yard, and that's why the man didn't give him full pay. But Rock Bottom worked any time the man could use him. He was making enough money to have something in his pocket all the time. He could buy what he wanted.

Rock Bottom liked everybody. Well, maybe he didn't like everybody the same way, but he sure didn't hate nobody. He worked with men, but he used to hang out with younger boys. Mostly he liked boys like fifteen and sixteen, and especially he liked little kids.

The men at the wrecking yard liked him. They would laugh at him when he was being funny, but they didn't laugh at the way he looked. And they didn't play him down, either, because they knew he carried his part of the job. The older men would warn him sometimes, tell him to be careful. They didn't want to see him get hurt, or hurt himself trying to do something he couldn't really do, like turning over a car or lifting too much.

The kids liked to hang around Rock Bottom. It was funny to see him going down the street with all the little kids around him. He would be walking, just walking real steady—swinging, kind of. Some of the kids would be ahead of him looking back, trying to talk to him, trying to do something to make him look at them. Some would be running along behind. Some would be changing from in front of him to in back of him. He would be just walking steady.

They liked to go down to the wrecking yard, too, but the man would drive them away. Then he would say if they didn't stay off the premises Rock Bottom would be fired. Nobody wanted that, so they would stay away for a day, or maybe two or three days. Then, when somebody wanted to look for a piece of iron to work on his wagon or something like that, they would be right back, and they would say they weren't there to see Rock Bottom but to do business.

The man that ran the wrecking yard didn't have all the big machines that some of the big yards had. Most of his work the men did with their hands and with their backs. That's where Rock Bottom came in. He was so strong he could move most anything, even better than men who were older than he was.

The older men would laugh and say, "Rock Bottom, that boy don't know his strength."

When the freight trains picked up scrap, they would have big cranes. The wrecking yard was right by a railroad siding. The big crane would reach over and pick up the scrap iron just like some big animal. It would swing over and drop the scrap in one of those open cars they call a gondola. The boys liked to watch them do that. Then sometimes they used a crane that had a big electric magnet. The steel and iron would just naturally stick on the magnet until the man who was running it swung the crane out over the gondola and cut off the juice. Then all the scrap would come down together.

John Berry, he was supposed to be real smart in general science and he told the boys about how it works.

"It's just plain magnetism," John Berry told us. "It's simple. Anybody could do it."

John wanted to get close.

"It can't hurt you," he told us. "You see, it's only metal. It can't hurt you," he said. "No electricity there. The juice is just in the coils. It's only the magnetic force."

Just the same, we were afraid to go near, and the man didn't like us to be anywhere around.

The man had air-conditioning in his office. He wouldn't come out when it was hot. And one day in the summer when it was too hot even to go swimming, they were loading steel and John Berry and Flemming and

Rock Bottom's cousin and some more of us stopped by to watch.

"It can't hurt you," John said. He started going over closer to the pile of scrap.

"It's got a fifty-thousand-volt magnetic force. But that's just a pull."

Johnny kept getting closer.

Next time the big magnet came low, he picked up a piece of scrap and he threw it at the magnet and it stuck right on the side and all the boys laughed.

"Watch this, now," he said. "I'm not even going to throw *at* it, just *by* it."

Then he threw a big bolt, not at the magnet. You could see it looked like it would miss it, but it curved right on around and hit it smack and stuck there. Everybody laughed, and when the magnet went up in the air again, everybody was throwing at the mess of scrap that was hanging down. And everything we threw even nearby, it would go over and smack against the rest of it and everything would stick.

Rock Bottom was standing on one end of the gondola. The magnet was coming down again when Rock Bottom saw the boys around the scrap pile, and he hollered, "You all get away from there. It's dangerous!"

We started backing away. We weren't really afraid, but then everybody liked Rock Bottom, anyway, and we didn't want to make any trouble for him. That is, everybody was backing away except John Berry.

John was sneaking up on the pile of scrap. He was sticking out his tongue from one corner of his mouth, and his face was twisted. You could see he had an idea to do something big.

The magnet was coming down like a bird. It settled down real easy, and the juice wasn't on because the scrap metal wasn't jumping around to stick on it.

John kind of climbed up on the side of the scrap pile. He was shoving a long twisted piece of steel at the magnet when the man turned on the juice, and all the scrap jumped and then froze onto the magnet and John Berry was caught. His hand was caught, jammed between the piece he was holding and some more scrap.

John didn't holler. That is, he didn't really holler. Maybe it wasn't hurting him. He just kind of hollered once. It was kind of a yelp, like a dog when he gets hit by a rock.

Then the magnet started up, and it carried John Berry with it.

In the gondola, Rock Bottom couldn't see John Berry when he got caught, but when John went up in the air, Rock Bottom saw him. He let out a yell. He was calling to the man in the cab, trying to make him see John Berry hanging up there in the scrap. The man couldn't hear, or he couldn't understand, and he couldn't see what was happening.

Rock Bottom started moving. He was fast, big as he was. He got right under the magnet. He was calling to John Berry. Maybe he thought John could just let go. It looked like he was going to catch the boy.

Then the man running the magnet cut the current. Later, he said he still hadn't seen John Berry, and he hadn't seen Rock Bottom in the gondola. He just knew he had position and he cut.

The scrap—big pieces and small—and John Berry all came down together.

For a little time the friends of John Berry and of Rock Bottom just stood. Then Rock Bottom's little cousin started screaming. The other workers in the wrecking yard went scrambling up into the gondola. The boss man came running from inside his air-conditioned office. He was cursing. One of the men in the gondola called to the man who ran the machine. He lowered the magnet, and then, together with the man who ran the yard and the men who were workers, they started lifting steel.

It didn't take long.

John Berry had a broken leg, and the wind was knocked out of him, with Rock Bottom on top of him and him grabbed in Rock Bottom's arms.

There was blood. John Berry was covered with blood. It was Rock Bottom's blood. A sharp piece of steel had sliced across Rock Bottom's neck just above the left shoulder. Rock Bottom was dead when they got to him.

They had a story in the paper. They said Robert Buttrick—that was his real name—was a hero. Mr. Peterson, the man who ran the wrecking yard, said Rock Bottom was a fool. Mrs. Wilson, John Berry's grandmother who was raising John Berry, she said Rock Bottom must have been an angel on earth, especially sent to do the will of God before going back to his angel duties in heaven.

Who's Who

A shilling life will give you all the facts:
How Father beat him, how he ran away,
What were the struggles of his youth, what acts
Made him the greatest figure of his day:

Of how he fought, fished, hunted, worked all night,
Though giddy, climbed new mountains; named a sea:

Some of the last researchers even write
Love made him weep his pints like you and me.

With all his honours on, he sighed for one
Who, say astonished critics, lived at home;
Did little jobs about the house with skill

And nothing else; could whistle; would sit still
Or potter round the garden; answered some
Of his long marvellous letters but kept none.

W. H. Auden

Compare with "Ex-Basketball Player" (p. 101). Is the "hero" of this poem another "Ex-Basketball Player"?

The Coming of the Teacher

Helen Keller

Helen Keller was less than two years old when she was stricken with a disease that left her deaf and blind, and for the next five years she remained in this dark, lonely world without even the ability to speak. Then came the great day when Anne Sullivan arrived from the Perkins Institute for the Blind.

The most important day I remember in all my life is the one on which my teacher, Anne Mansfield Sullivan, came to me. I am filled with wonder when I consider the immeasurable contrast between the two lives which it connects. It was the third of March, 1887, three months before I was seven years old.

On the afternoon of that eventful day, I stood on the porch, dumb, expectant. I guessed vaguely from my mother's signs and from the hurrying to and fro in the house that something unusual was about to happen; so I went to the door and waited on the steps. The afternoon sun penetrated the mass of honeysuckle that covered the porch, and fell on my upturned face. My fingers lingered almost unconsciously on the familiar leaves and blossoms which had just come forth to greet the sweet Southern spring. I did not know what the future held of marvel or surprise for me. Anger and bitterness had preyed upon me continually for weeks, and a deep languor had succeeded this passionate struggle.

Have you ever been at sea in a dense fog, when it seemed as if a tangible white darkness shut you in, and the great ship, tense and anxious, groped her way toward the shore with plummet and sounding line, and you waited with beating heart for something to happen? I was like that ship before my education began, only I was without compass or sounding line, and had no way of knowing how near the harbor was. "Light! Give me light!" was the wordless cry of my soul, and the light of love shone on me in that very hour.

I felt approaching footsteps. I stretched out my hand as I supposed to my mother. Someone took it, and I was caught up and held close in the arms of her who had come to reveal all things to me, and, more than all things else, to love me.

The morning after my teacher came she led me into her room and gave me a doll. The little blind children at the Perkins Institution had sent it, and Laura Bridgman had dressed it; but I did not know this until afterward.

When I had played with it a little while, Miss Sullivan slowly spelled into my hand the word "d-o-l-l." I was at once interested in this finger play and tried to imitate it. When I finally succeeded in making the letters correctly, I was flushed with childish pleasure and pride. Running downstairs to my mother, I held up my hand and made the letters for *doll.* I did not know that I was spelling a word or even that words existed; I was simply making my fingers go in monkeylike imitation. In the days that followed I learned to spell in this uncomprehending way a great many words, among them *pin, hat, cup* and a few verbs like *sit, stand,* and *walk.* But my teacher had been with me several weeks before I understood that everything has a name.

One day, while I was playing with my new doll, Miss Sullivan put my big rag doll into my lap also, spelled "d-o-l-l" and tried to make me understand that "d-o-l-l" applied to both. Earlier in the day we had had a tussle over the words "m-u-g" and "w-a-t-e-r." Miss Sullivan had tried to impress it upon me that "m-u-g" is *mug* and that "w-a-t-e-r" is *water,* but I persisted in confounding the two. In despair she had dropped the subject for the time, only to renew it at the first opportunity. I became impatient at her repeated attempts and, seizing the new doll, I dashed it upon the floor. I was keenly delighted when I felt the fragments of the broken doll at my feet. Neither sorrow nor regret followed my passionate outburst. I had not loved the doll. In the still, dark world in which I lived there was no strong sentiment or tenderness. I felt my teacher sweep the fragments to one side of the hearth, and I had a sense of satisfaction that the cause of my discomfort was removed. She brought me my hat, and I knew I was going out into the warm sunshine. This thought, if a wordless sensation may be called a thought, made me hop and skip with pleasure.

We walked down the path to the well-house, attracted by the fragrance of the honeysuckle with which it was covered. Someone was drawing water, and my teacher placed my hand under the spout. As the cool stream gushed over one hand, she spelled into the other the word *water,* first slowly, then rapidly. I stood still, my whole attention fixed upon the motions of her fingers. Suddenly I felt a misty consciousness as of something forgotten—a thrill of returning thought; and somehow the mystery of language was revealed to me. I knew then that "w-a-t-e-r" meant the wonderful cool something that was flowing over my hand. That living word awakened my soul, gave it light, hope, joy, set it free! There were barriers still, it is true, but barriers that could in time be swept away.

I left the well-house eager to learn. Everything had a name, and each name gave birth to a new thought. As we returned to the house, every object which I touched seemed to quiver with life. That was because I saw everything with the strange, new sight that had come to me. On entering the door, I remembered the doll I had broken. I felt my way to the hearth and picked up the pieces. I tried vainly to put them together. Then my eyes filled with tears; for I realized what I had done, and for the first time I felt repentance and sorrow.

I learned a great many new words that day. I do not remember what they all were; but I do know that *mother, father, sister, teacher* were among them—words that were to make the world blossom for me, "like Aaron's rod, with flowers." It would have been difficult to find a happier child than I was as I lay in my crib at the close of that eventful day and lived over the joys it had brought me, and for the first time longed for a new day to come.

Carlozini

N. Scott Momaday

Old Carlozini ought to be getting home pretty soon. She's old, and she ought not to be out in the rain like that. One of these days she's going to just fall down and die in the street, or they're going to find her all alone in that little room of hers. She has a few little things, you know, some dishes and spoons, and every morning about five-thirty you can hear her moving around down there.

She always wears that old black hat when she goes out. It looks funny on her because it's big and the brim droops down all around her head and there's an old beat-up flower that hangs down over one eye and bounces around when she walks. She never says hello or anything, but she's always watching you, like maybe she thinks you're going to sneak up on her or steal something from her. She can hear you on the stairs, you know, and she always opens her door a little, just a crack, and watches you go by. That's about all she has to do, I guess.

One time we were going out, and old Carlozini was sitting down there on the stairs, all bent over and still, like she was going to sleep. The door of her room was wide open, and she was just sitting out there on the stairs, and it was the first time we had ever seen the inside of her room. It was real dark and dirty-looking, and even out there on the stairs we could smell it. I guess it was the first time that door had ever been left open like that. She never takes a bath, and you know how old people smell and how they like to shut themselves up in the dark. It was pretty bad, that smell.

Well, we started to go around her and she said something. We turned and she was looking up at us and her eyes were all wet. "Vincenzo is not well," she said. "It is very bad this time." She had a little cardboard box in her hands and she held it out to us.

We didn't know what she was talking about, but we looked inside that box and there was a little dead animal of some kind, a guinea pig, I guess; it had black and white fur and it was kind of curled up on its side and there was a dirty white cloth under it.

"Oh, it is very bad this time," she said, and she was shaking her head. We didn't know what to say, and she was crying and looking at us like maybe we could make it all right if we wanted to. It was like she was being real friendly and nice to us, you know, so we would make it all right.

"His name is Vincenzo," she said. "He's very smart, you know; he can stand up straight, just like you gentlemen, and clap his little hands." And her eyes lit up and she had to smile, thinking about it. She went on like that, like that little thing was still alive and maybe it was going to stand up and clap its hands like a baby.

It made me real sad to see her, so old and lonely and carrying on like that, and she kept saying "you gentlemen" and everything. We didn't know what to do, and we just listened to her and looked down at that little furry animal. And then after a while my friend said he thought it was dead. At first I thought he shouldn't have said that; it seemed kind of mean somehow, you know? But I guess she had to be told. I think maybe she knew it was dead all the time, and she was just waiting for someone to say it, because she didn't know how to say it herself.

All at once she jerked that little box away and looked at him real hard for a minute, like she was hurt and couldn't understand how it was, why on earth he should say a thing like that. But then she just nodded and slumped over a little bit. She didn't say any more, and she wasn't crying; it was like she was real tired, you know, and didn't have any strength left. I asked her if she wanted us to take Vincenzo out to the alley, but she just sat there and didn't say anything.

She was just sitting there on the stairs, holding that little dead animal real close to her, and she looked awful small and alone and the night was coming on and it was getting dark down there. It's funny, you know; that little animal was her friend, I guess, and she kept it down there in her room, always, maybe, and we didn't even know about it. And afterward it was just the same. She never said anything to us again.

Can you name a "Carlozini" that you know? Do you have the same feelings toward her as "I" does in this story?

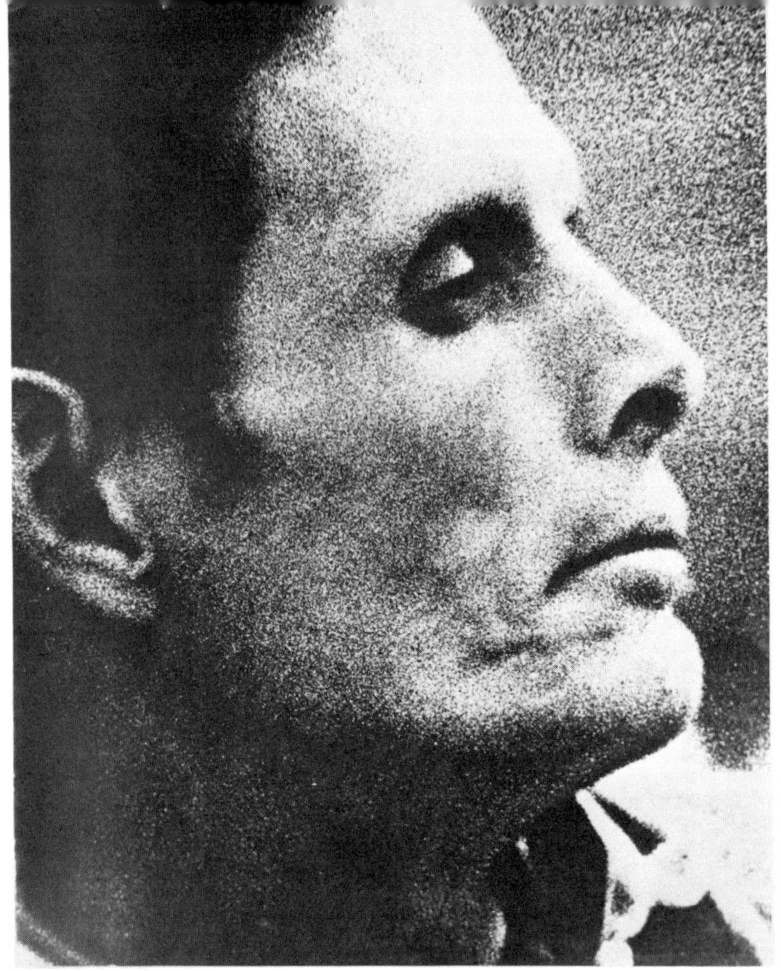

Unwanted

The poster with my picture on it
Is hanging on the bulletin board in the Post Office.

I stand by it hoping to be recognized
Posing first full face and then profile

But everybody passes by and I have to admit
The photograph was taken some years ago.

I was unwanted then and I'm unwanted now
Ah guess ah'll go up echo mountain and crah.

I wish someone would find my fingerprints somewhere
Maybe on a corpse and say, You're it.

Description: Male, or reasonably so
White, but not lily-white and usually deep-red

Thirty fivish, and looks it lately
Five-feet-nine and one-hundred-thirty pounds: no
physique

Black hair going gray, hairline receding fast
What used to be curly, now fuzzy

Brown eyes starey under beetling brow
Mole on chin, probably will become a wen

It is perfectly obvious that he was not popular at school
No good at baseball, and wet his bed.

His aliases tell his history: Dumbell, Good-for-nothing,
Jewboy, Fieldinsky, Skinny, Fierce Face, Greaseball,
Sissy.

Warning: This man is not dangerous, answers to any
name
Responds to love, don't call him or he will come.

Edward Field

What do you usually think of when you see "Wanted" posters? How is the poet's portrait different from the government's?

A Name on the Wall

Robert Marmorstein

Steve Mason had lived in New York for three years. His address book was filled with the phone numbers of girls he knew and had dated. Then why, he wondered, was he sitting in a phone booth about to dial PL 1-2450—the phone number of a girl he had never seen or even heard about?

Because he was curious.

He had seen the name Pam Starr and the number PL 1-2450 twice in one week. The first time had been on the wall of a phone booth on 42nd Street. It was just one of the many names and numbers written on the phone-booth wall. Then a minute ago he had seen the name and number again—this time near a phone in a drugstore. The name Pam Starr was the same. The handwriting was the same. And beneath it the same person had written, "Quite a chick."

Steve was so curious that he looked up the name in the telephone book. There it was—Pam Starr, PLaza 1-2450. He was so surprised to see the name and number actually in the telephone book that he decided to call.

Probably the whole thing was a gag or a set-up for something crooked. But Steve thought he would take a chance. He wanted to find out what would happen when he called. He could hear himself telling the whole story to his friends and laughing about it when it was over. It would be an interesting adventure. So he took a deep breath, dropped in his dime, and dialed PL 1-2450.

He heard two rings; then a soft, pleasant, girl's voice said, "Hello."

"May I speak to Pam Starr?" Steve asked.

"This is Pam," she answered. "Who is this?"

"Steven Wordsley," he said, using a phony name to protect himself just in case something really tricky was going on. "You don't know me," he added quickly. "I just moved to New York from Chicago. But before I left, a friend of a friend of mine gave me your name. For the life of me, I can't remember this guy's name, but he told me to look you up when I got to New York and maybe get together with you for a drink."

The girl hesitated. "It's impossible for me to know much about you from a phone call."

"That's right," Steve said. "But there's no way for you to find out about me except by taking a chance. So how about a date?" He paused. "Come on. Gamble. I swear I don't have two heads."

She laughed and said, "I'm sure you don't. But I've had a couple of blind dates before, and they've been pretty gruesome, if you know what I mean."

Steve had a good idea of what she meant. He could picture this gorgeous doll getting stuck with some real dog for a date.

Then she said, "I've got an idea. I like your voice, and I think I'd like you. But I might not. And then again, you might not like me. So why don't we go to a movie? I like foreign ones best. You pick one out and call me back. Then we'll go out, and even if we can't stand each other, at least we can both enjoy the show."

"Uh, all right, sure," Steve answered. He was a little surprised by the way she was taking over arranging the date, but he promised to pick out a movie and call her back. Then he said good-by and hung up. He felt proud of himself. There was no question in his mind that this chick knew her way around with men.

Steve found a Swedish movie that sounded good, but he didn't call her back right away. He waited two days so he wouldn't seem too eager. Then he called and made a date for the next Saturday evening.

At seven-thirty Saturday night Steve went to her address. For a moment he wondered why he had gotten himself into this spot. The whole thing could be some sort of racket, or he could be stuck with a witch for a date. But he was too curious to give up now. So he went into the small lobby and rang the bell for apartment 312. She buzzed back to open the inside door. He took an elevator to the third floor and knocked on the door of her apartment.

She opened the door, and Steve knew he was a loser.

The girl had tried to make herself look attractive, but she couldn't hide her homeliness. She wasn't really ugly, but she was no gorgeous chick.

She smiled weakly at Steve, and he couldn't be sure if it was to apologize for her looks or to hide her fear that he might turn around and walk away.

Steve covered up his disappointment with a friendly smile. "Hello, Pam. I'm Steve."

She laughed and said, "I know I'm not the most beautiful girl in the world, but—"

"I wasn't looking for the most beautiful girl in the world," Steve lied. "Come on, let's go see the movie."

He smiled as cheerfully as he could. He had taken a chance on a blind date and had lost, but he decided to go through with it, anyway. This homely girl was obviously someone who accepted a lot of blind dates just so she could go out. And the guys who got stuck with her probably thought it was a good joke to write her name and number on the walls of phone booths. Still, the girl did seem nice, and the adventure would be something he could tell his friends.

As they headed for the movie, Steve expected Pam to

be nervous and try very hard to be a "fun" date. But she acted as relaxed as if she had been dating him for months.

After the show they went to a restaurant. While they were eating, she talked about her life in New York.

"Do you go out often?" Steve asked. "I mean, I hear it's a problem for girls alone in New York. It's tough to meet single people in the big city."

"Oh, I have my share of dates," she said. "It's probably luck but I get enough phone calls to keep me busy. I *do* get a lot of calls from guys I don't know. I'm not sure where they get my name. Maybe from a friend, like you did. I don't know. Some are nice and some aren't."

"Well, which am I?" Steve asked.

"Nice," she laughed.

On their way back to her apartment, Steve lied again and told Pam that his company was sending him back to Chicago the next week and that he didn't know when he would return to New York. Steve couldn't decide if she believed his story, but he didn't really care. He had taken her out and shown her a good time. That was all she could expect with her looks.

When they got to her apartment, they stood in the doorway and said good night.

"Thanks for a lovely evening," she said.

"Yeah," Steve said, "it was a good movie."

She smiled and said, "I enjoyed it. I really did." She seemed to know that she would not be asked for another date.

Suddenly Steve felt very sorry for her. He decided that it wouldn't hurt him to fake an interest in her, and it would probably mean a lot to her if she thought *someone* wanted to see her again.

"I'm kind of sorry I have to leave town," he said. "I really would have liked to see you again. There's just a chance that I'll get back to New York soon. For a day or so. Maybe we can go out again. Could I call you?"

For a minute she looked as if she didn't believe what she had heard. Then her smile got brighter. "Could you? I'd love that! I'd love to have you call. Do you think they'll send you back soon?"

"Sure, sure, you never know," Steve said. "And when I get back here, I'll *definitely* call."

"I'd be so happy to hear from you," she said. "You won't lose my number, will you? I'm in the phone book if you do. But if you're here only for a day you could call me at my office. Yes, better call me there. I'll write down my office number for you right now. Wait just a second."

She ran into her apartment to get a pencil and some paper. As she ripped a sheet from a pad of paper, she dropped the pencil on the floor. She got down on her hands and knees and scrambled after the rolling pencil. Finally she grabbed the pencil and then quickly wrote her name and office phone number.

Steve watched her sadly. Even before she handed him the piece of paper, he knew that her handwriting would be the same as the handwriting on the phone-booth walls.

Miss Brill

Katherine Mansfield

Although it was so brilliantly fine—the blue sky powdered with gold and great spots of light like white wine splashed over the Jardins Publiques—Miss Brill was glad that she had decided on her fur. The air was motionless, but when you opened your mouth there was just a faint chill, like the chill from a glass of iced water before you sip, and now and again a leaf came drifting—from nowhere, from the sky.

Miss Brill put up her hand and touched her fur. Dear little thing! It was nice to feel it again. She had taken it out of its box that afternoon, shaken out the moth powder, given it a good brush, and rubbed the life back into the dim little eyes. "What has been happening to me?" said the sad little eyes. Oh, how sweet it was to see them snap at her again from the red eider down! . . . But the nose, which was of some black composition, wasn't at all firm. It must have had a knock, somehow. Never mind—a little dab of black sealing wax when the time came—when it was absolutely necessary. . . . Little rogue! Yes, she really felt like that about it. Little rogue biting its tail just by her left ear. She could have taken it off and laid it on her lap and stroked it. She felt a tingling in her hands and arms, but that came from walking, she supposed. And when she breathed, something light and sad—no, not sad, exactly—something gentle seemed to move in her bosom.

There were a number of people out this afternoon, far more than last Sunday. And the band sounded louder and gayer. That was because the Season had begun. For although the band played all the year round on Sundays, out of season it was never the same. It was like someone playing with only the family to listen; it didn't care how it played if there weren't any strangers present. Wasn't the conductor wearing a new coat, too? She was sure it was new. He scraped with his foot and flapped his arms like a rooster about to crow, and the bandsmen sitting in the green rotunda blew out their cheeks and glared at the music. Now there came a little "flutey" bit—very pretty!—a little chain of bright drops.

She was sure it would be repeated. It was; she lifted her head and smiled.

Only two people shared her "special" seat; a fine old man in a velvet coat, his hands clasped over a huge carved walking stick, and a big old woman, sitting upright, with a roll of knitting on her embroidered apron. They did not speak. This was disappointing, for Miss Brill always looked forward to the conversation. She had become really quite expert, she thought, at listening as though she didn't listen, at sitting in other people's lives just for a minute while they talked round her.

She glanced, sideways, at the old couple. Perhaps they would go soon. Last Sunday, too, hadn't been as interesting as usual. An Englishman and his wife, he wearing a dreadful Panama hat and she button boots. And she'd gone on the whole time about how she ought to wear spectacles; she knew she needed them; but that it was no good getting any; they'd be sure to break and they'd never keep on. And he'd been so patient. He'd suggested everything–gold rims, the kind that curved around your ears, little pads inside the bridge. No, nothing would please her. "They'll always be sliding down my nose!" Miss Brill had wanted to shake her.

The old people sat on the bench, still as statues. Never mind, there was always the crowd to watch. To and fro, in front of the flower beds and the band rotunda, the couples and groups paraded, stopped to talk, to greet, to buy a handful of flowers from the old beggar who had his tray fixed to the railings. Little children ran among them, swooping and laughing; little boys with big white silk bows under their chins, little girls, little French dolls, dressed up in velvet and lace. And sometimes a tiny staggerer came suddenly rocking into the open from under the trees, stopped, stared, as suddenly sat down "flop," until its small high-stepping mother, like a young hen, rushed scolding to its rescue. Other people sat on the benches and green chairs, but they were nearly always the same, Sunday after Sunday, and—Miss Brill had often noticed—there was something funny about nearly all of them. They were odd, silent, nearly all old, and from the way they stared they looked as though they'd just come from dark little rooms or even—even cupboards.

Behind the rotunda the slender trees with yellow leaves down drooping, and through them just a line of sea, and beyond the blue sky with gold-veined clouds.

Tum-tum-tum tiddle-um! tiddle-um! tum tiddley-um tum ta! blew the band.

Two young girls in red came by and two young soldiers in blue met them, and they laughed and paired and went off arm in arm. Two peasant women with funny straw hats passed, gravely, leading beautiful smoke-colored donkeys. A cold, pale nun hurried by. A beautiful woman came along and dropped her bunch of violets, and a little boy ran after to hand them to her, and she took them and threw them away as if they'd been poisoned. Dear me! Miss Brill didn't know whether to admire that or not!

And now an ermine toque and a gentleman in gray met just in front of her. He was tall, stiff, dignified, and she was wearing the ermine toque she'd bought when her hair was yellow. Now everything, her hair, her face, even her eyes, was the same color as the shabby ermine, and her hand in its cleaned glove, lifted to dab her lips, with a tiny yellowish paw. Oh, she was so pleased to see him—delighted! She rather thought they were going to meet that afternoon. She described where she'd been—everywhere, here, there, along by the sea. The day was so charming—didn't he agree? And wouldn't he, perhaps? . . . But he shook his head—lighted a cigarette, slowly breathed a great deep puff into her face, and, even while she was still talking and laughing, flicked the match away and walked on. The ermine toque was alone; she smiled more brightly than ever. But even the band seemed to know what she was feeling and played more softly, played tenderly, and the drum beat, "The Brute! The Brute!" over and over. What would she do? What was going to happen now? But as Miss Brill wondered, the ermine toque turned, raised her hand as though she'd seen someone else, much nicer, just over there, and pattered away. And the band changed again and played more quickly, more gaily than ever, and the old couple on Miss Brill's seat got up and marched away, and such a funny old man with long whiskers hobbled along in time to the music and was nearly knocked over by four girls walking abreast.

Oh, how fascinating it was! How she enjoyed it! How she loved sitting here, watching it all! It was like a play. It was exactly like a play. Who could believe the sky at the back wasn't painted? But it wasn't till a little brown dog trotted on solemnly and then slowly trotted off, like a little "theater" dog, a little dog that had been drugged, that Miss Brill discovered what it was that made it so exciting. They were all on the stage. They weren't only the audience, not only looking on; they were acting. Even she had a part and came every Sunday. No doubt somebody would have noticed if she hadn't been there; she was part of the performance after all.

How strange she'd never thought of it like that before! And yet it explained why she made such a point of starting from home at just the same time each week—so as not to be late for the performance—and it also explained why she had quite a queer, shy feeling at telling her English pupils how she spent her Sunday afternoons.

No wonder! Miss Brill nearly laughed out loud. She was on the stage. She thought of the old invalid gentleman to whom she read the newspaper four afternoons a week while he slept in the garden. She had got quite used to the frail head on the cotton pillow, the hollowed eyes, the open mouth and the high pinched nose. If he'd been dead she mightn't have noticed for weeks; she wouldn't have minded. But suddenly he knew he was having the paper read to him by an actress! "An actress!" The old head lifted; two points of light quivered in the old eyes. "An actress—are ye?" And Miss Brill smoothed the newspaper as though it were the manuscript of her part and said gently: "Yes, I have been an actress for a long time."

The band had been having a rest. Now they started again. And what they played was warm, sunny, yet there was just a faint chill—a something, what was it?—not sadness—no, not sadness—a something that made you want to sing. The tune lifted, lifted, the light shone; and it seemed to Miss Brill that in another moment all of them, all the whole company, would begin singing. The young ones, the laughing ones who were moving together, they would begin, and the men's voices, very resolute and brave, would join them. And then she too, she too, and the others on the benches—they would come in with a kind of accompaniment—something low, that scarcely rose or fell, something so beautiful—moving. . . . And Miss Brill's eyes filled with tears and she looked smiling at all the other members of the company. Yes, we understand, we understand, she thought—though what they understood she didn't know.

Just at that moment a boy and girl came and sat down where the old couple had been. They were beautifully dressed; they were in love. The hero and heroine, of course, just arrived from his father's yacht. And still soundlessly singing, still with that trembling smile. Miss Brill prepared to listen.

"No, not now," said the girl. "Not here, I can't."

"But why? Because of that stupid old thing at the end there?" asked the boy. "Why does she come here at all—who wants her? Why doesn't she keep her silly old mug at home?"

"It's her fu-fur which is so funny," giggled the girl. "It's exactly like a fried whiting."

"Ah, be off with you!" said the boy in an angry whisper. Then: "Tell me, *ma petite chérie—*"

"No, not here," said the girl. "Not *yet.*"

On her way home she usually bought a slice of honeycake at the baker's. It was her Sunday treat. Sometimes there was an almond in her slice, sometimes not. It made a great difference. If there was an almond, it was like carrying home a tiny present—a surprise—something that might very well not have been there. She hurried on the almond Sundays and struck the match for the kettle in quite a dashing way.

But today she passed the baker's by, climbed the stairs, went into the little dark room—her room like a cupboard—and sat down on the red eider down. She sat there for a long time. The box that the fur came out of was on the bed. She unclasped the necklet quickly; quickly, without looking, laid it inside. But when she put the lid on she thought she heard something crying.

Ex-Basketball Player

Pearl Avenue runs past the high school lot,
Bends with the trolley tracks, and stops, cut off
Before it has a chance to go two blocks,
At Colonel McComsky Plaza. Berth's Garage
Is on the corner facing west, and there,
Most days, you'll find Flick Webb, who helps Berth out.

Flick stands tall among the idiot pumps—
Five on a side, the old bubble-head style,
Their rubber elbows hanging loose and low.
One's nostrils are two S's, and his eyes
An E and O. And one is squat, without
A head at all—more of a football type.

Once, Flick played for the high school team, the
 Wizards.
He was good: in fact, the best. In '46,
He bucketed three hundred ninety points,
A county record still. The ball loved Flick.
I saw him rack up thirty-eight or forty
In one home game. His hands were like wild birds.

He never learned a trade; he just sells gas,
Checks oil, and changes flats. Once in a while,
As a gag, he dribbles an inner tube,
But most of us remember anyway.
His hands are fine and nervous on the lug wrench.
It makes no difference to the lug wrench, though.

Off work, he hangs around Mae's Luncheonette.
Grease-grey and kind of coiled, he plays pinball,

Sips lemon cokes, and smokes those thin cigars;
Flick seldom speaks to Mae, just sits and nods
Beyond her face towards bright applauding tiers
Of Necco Wafers, Nibs, and Juju Beads.

John Updike

Why did Flick fail?

Who is responsible?

The Miner

Those on the top say they know you, Earth—they are
liars.
You are my father, and the silence I work in is my
mother.
Only the son knows his father.
We are alike—sweaty, inarticulate of soul, bending under
thick knowledge.
I drink and shout with my brothers when above you—
Like most children we soon forget the parents of our
souls.
But you avidly grip us again—we pay for the little noise
of life we steal.

Maxwell Bodenheim

What similarities between the earth and the miner has the poet perceived? Is it a convincing comparison? How would your response be different if you had ever been in a mine or a deep cave?

The Market Man

The walnut brains think moist
in their light tan skulls;
the apples croon redly
of their tooth white pulp;
and the squash curves voluptuously
in its yellow skin.

It is cold and the market man
burns an orange crate;
it is dark and bare bulbs hang down
like fiery glass pears.
The market man has big blunt thumbs,
he feels chapped melons;
the market man has a strong mouth,
dry as potato dust;
the market man has black grape eyes,
no seeds show in them.
The market man has lonely shanks,
he splats lemons against a wall;
the market man is angry at the cold,
he strips the heads of lettuce down
and throws the green leaves on the cobble street;
the market man smells the salty river,
he bites an onion open with his teeth
and floods the black night with tears and burning.

John Ratti

Shane

Jack Schaefer

He rode into our valley in the summer of '89. I was a kid then, barely topping the backboard of father's old chuck-wagon. I was on the upper rail of our small corral, soaking in the late afternoon sun, when I saw him far down the road where it swung into the valley from the open plain beyond.

In that clear Wyoming air I could see him plainly, though he was still several miles away. There seemed nothing remarkable about him, just another stray horseman riding up the road toward the cluster of frame buildings that was our town. Then I saw a pair of cowhands, loping past him, stop and stare after him with a curious intentness.

He came steadily on, straight through the town without slackening pace, until he reached the fork a half-mile below our place. One branch turned left across the river ford and on to Luke Fletcher's big spread. The other bore ahead along the right bank where we homesteaders had pegged our claims in a row up the valley. He hesitated briefly, studying the choice, and moved again steadily on our side.

As he came near, what impressed me first was his clothes. He wore dark trousers of some serge materials tucked into tall boots and held at the waist by a wide belt, both of a soft black leather tooled in intricate design. A coat of the same dark material as the trousers was neatly folded and strapped to his saddle-roll. His shirt was finespun linen, rich brown in color. The handkerchief knotted loosely around his throat was black silk. His hat was not the familiar Stetson, not the familiar gray or muddy tan. It was a plain black, soft in texture, unlike any hat I had ever seen, with a creased crown and a wide curling brim swept down in front to shield the face.

All trace of newness was long since gone from these things. The dust of distance was beaten into them. They were worn and stained and several neat patches showed on the shirt. Yet a kind of magnificence remained and with it a hint of men and manners alien to my limited boy's experience.

Then I forgot the clothes in the impact of the man himself. He was not much above medium height, almost slight in build. He would have looked frail alongside father's square, solid bulk. But even I could read the endurance in the lines of that dark figure and the quiet power in its effortless, unthinking adjustment to every movement of the tired horse.

He was clean-shaven and his face was lean and hard and burned from high forehead to firm, tapering chin. His eyes seemed hooded in the shadow of the hat's brim. He came closer, and I could see that this was because the brows were drawn in a frown of fixed and habitual alertness. Beneath them the eyes were endlessly searching from side to side and forward, checking off every item in view, missing nothing. As I noticed this, a sudden chill, I could not have told why, struck through me there in the warm and open sun.

He rode easily, relaxed in the saddle, leaning his weight lazily into the stirrups. Yet even in this easiness was a suggestion of tension. It was the easiness of a coiled spring, of a trap set.

He drew rein not twenty feet from me. His glance hit me, dismissed me, flickered over our place. This was not much, if you were thinking in terms of size and scope. But what there was was good. You could trust father for that. The corral, big enough for about thirty head if you crowded them in, was railed right to true sunk posts. The pasture behind, taking in nearly half of our claim, was fenced tight. The barn was small, but it was solid, and we were raising a loft at one end for the alfalfa growing green in the north forty. We had a fair-sized field in potatoes that year and father was trying a new corn he had sent all the way to Washington for and they were showing properly in weedless rows.

Behind the house, mother's kitchen garden was a brave sight. The house itself was three rooms—two really, the big kitchen where we spent most of our time indoors and the bedroom beside it. My little lean-to room was added back of the kitchen. Father was planning, when he could get around to it, to build mother the parlor she wanted.

We had wooden floors and a nice porch across the front. The house was painted too, white with green trim, rare thing in all that region, to remind her, mother said when she made father do it, of her native New England. Even rarer, the roof was shingled. I knew what that meant. I had helped father split those shingles. Few places so spruce and well worked could be found so deep in the Territory in those days.

The stranger took it all in, sitting there easily in the saddle. I saw his eyes slow on the flowers mother had planted by the porch steps, then come to rest on our shiny new pump and the trough beside it. They shifted back to me, and again, without knowing why, I felt that sudden chill. But his voice was gentle and he spoke like a man schooled in patience.

"I'd appreciate a chance at the pump for myself and the horse."

I was trying to frame a reply and choking on it, when

I realized that he was not speaking to me but past me. Father had come up behind me and was leaning against the gate to the corral.

"Use all the water you want, stranger."

Father and I watched him dismount in a single flowing tilt of his body and lead the horse over to the trough. He pumped it almost full and let the horse sink its nose in the cool water before he picked up the dipper for himself.

He took his hat off and slapped the dust out of it and hung it on a corner of the trough. With his hands he brushed the dust from his clothes. With a piece of rag pulled from his saddle-roll he carefully wiped his boots. He untied the handkerchief from around his neck and rolled his sleeves and dipped his arms in the trough, rubbing thoroughly and splashing water over his face. He shook his hands dry and used the handkerchief to remove the last drops from his face. Taking a comb from his shirt pocket, he smoothed back his long dark hair. All his movements were deft and sure, and with a quick precision he flipped down his sleeves, reknotted the handkerchief, and picked up his hat.

Then, holding it in his hand, he spun about and strode directly toward the house. He bent low and snapped the stem of one of mother's petunias and tucked this into the hatband. In another moment the hat was on his head, brim swept down in swift, unconscious gesture, and he was swinging gracefully into the saddle and starting toward the road.

I was fascinated. None of the men I knew were proud like that about their appearance. In that short time the kind of magnificence I had noticed had emerged into plainer view. It was in the very air of him. Everything about him showed the effects of long use and hard use, but showed too the strength of quality and competence.

There was no chill on me now. Already I was imagining myself in that hat and belt and boots like those.

He stopped the horse and looked down at us. He was refreshed and I would have sworn the tiny wrinkles around his eyes were what with him would be a smile. His eyes were not restless when he looked at you like this. They were still and steady and you knew the man's whole attention was concentrated on you even in the casual glance.

"Thank you," he said in his gentle voice and was turning into the road, back to us, before father spoke in his slow, deliberate way.

"Don't be in such a hurry, stranger."

I had to hold tight to the rail or I would have fallen backwards into the corral. At the first sound of father's voice, the man and the horse, like a single being, had wheeled to face us, the man's eyes boring at father, bright and deep in the shadow of the hat's brim. I was shivering, struck through once more. Something intangible and cold and terrifying was there in the air between us.

I stared in wonder as father and the stranger looked at each other a long moment, measuring each other in an unspoken fraternity of adult knowledge beyond my reach. Then the warm sunlight was flooding over us, for father was smiling and he was speaking with the drawling emphasis that meant he had made up his mind.

"I said don't be in such a hurry, stranger. Food will be on the table soon and you can bed down here tonight."

The stranger nodded quietly as if he too had made up his mind. "That's mighty thoughtful of you," he said and swung down and came toward us, leading his horse. Father slipped into step beside him and we all headed for the barn.

"My name's Starrett," said father. "Joe Starrett. This here," waving at me, "is Robert MacPherson Starrett. Too much name for a boy. I make it Bob."

The stranger nodded again. "Call me Shane," he said. Then to me: "Bob it is. You were watching me for quite a spell coming up the road."

It was not a question. It was a simple statement. "Yes . . ." I stammered. "Yes. I was."

"Right," he said. "I like that. A man who watches what's going on around him will make his mark."

A man who watches . . . For all his dark appearance and lean, hard look, this Shane knew what would please a boy. The glow of it held me as he took care of his horse, and I fussed around, hanging up his saddle, forking over some hay, getting in his way and my own way in my eagerness. He let me slip the bridle off and the horse, bigger and more powerful than I had thought now that I was close beside it, put its head down patiently for me and stood quietly while I helped him curry away the caked dust. Only once did he stop me. That was when I reached for his saddle-roll to put it to one side. In the instant my fingers touched it, he was taking it from me and he put it on a shelf with a finality that indicated no interference.

When the three of us went up to the house, mother was waiting and four places were set at the table. "I saw you through the window," she said and came to shake our visitor's hand. She was a slender, lively woman with a fair complexion even our weather never seemed to affect and a mass of light brown hair she wore piled high to bring her, she used to say, closer to father's size.

"Marian," father said, "I'd like you to meet Mr. Shane."

"Good evening, ma'am," said our visitor. He took her hand and bowed over it. Mother stepped back and, to my surprise, dropped in a dainty curtsy. I had never seen her do that before. She was an unpredictable woman. Father and I would have painted the house three times over and in rainbow colors to please her.

"And a good evening to you, Mr. Shane. If Joe hadn't called you back, I would have done it myself. You'd never find a decent meal up the valley."

She was proud of her cooking, was mother. That was one thing she learned back home, she would often say, that was of some use out in this raw land. As long as she could still prepare a proper dinner, she would tell father when things were not going right, she knew she was civilized and there was hope of getting ahead. Then she would tighten up her lips and whisk together her special most delicious biscuits and father would watch her bustling about and eat them to the last little crumb and stand up and wipe his eyes and stretch his big frame and stomp out to his always unfinished work like daring anything to stop him.

We sat down to supper and a good one. Mother's eyes sparkled as our visitor kept pace with father and me. Then we all leaned back and while I listened the talk ran on almost like old friends around a familiar table. But I could sense that it was following a pattern. Father was trying, with mother helping and both of them avoiding direct questions, to get hold of facts about this Shane and he was dodging at every turn. He was aware of their purpose and not in the least annoyed by it. He was mild and courteous and spoke readily enough. But always he put them off with words that gave no real information.

He must have been riding many days, for he was full of news from towns along his back trail as far as Cheyenne and even Dodge City and others beyond I had never heard of before. But he had no news about himself. His past was fenced as tightly as our pasture. All they could learn was that he was riding through, taking each day as it came, with nothing particular in mind except maybe seeing a part of the country he had not been in before.

Afterwards mother washed the dishes and I dried and the two men sat on the porch, their voices carrying through the open door. Our visitor was guiding the conversation now and in no time at all he had father talking about his own plans. That was no trick. Father was ever one to argue his ideas whenever he could find a listener. This time he was going strong.

"Yes, Shane, the boys I used to ride with don't see it yet. They will some day. The open range can't last forever. The fence lines are closing in. Running cattle in big lots is good business only for the top ranchers and it's really a poor business at that. Poor in terms of the resources going into it. Too much space for too little results. It's certain to be crowded out."

"Well, now," said Shane, "That's mighty interesting. I've been hearing the same quite a lot lately and from men with pretty clear heads. Maybe there's something to it."

* * *

The dishes were done and I was edging to the door. Mother nailed me as she usually did and shunted me off to bed. After she had left me in my little back room and went to join the men on the porch, I tried to catch more of the words. The voices were too low. Then I must have dozed, for with a start I realized that father and mother were again in the kitchen. By now, I gathered, our visitor was out in the barn in the bunk father had built there for the hired man who had been with us for a few weeks in the spring.

"Wasn't it peculiar," I heard mother say, "how he wouldn't talk about himself?"

"Peculiar?" said father. "Well, yes. In a way."

"Everything about him is peculiar." Mother sounded as if she was stirred up and interested. "I never saw a man quite like him before."

"You wouldn't have. Not where you come from. He's a special brand we sometimes get out here in the grass country. I've come across a few. A bad one's poison. A good one's straight grain clear through."

"How can you be so sure about him? Why, he wouldn't even tell where he was raised."

"Born back east a ways would be my guess. And pretty far south. Tennessee maybe. But he's been around plenty."

"I like him." Mother's voice was serious. "He's so nice and polite and sort of gentle. Not like most men I've met out here. But there's something about him. Something underneath the gentleness . . . Something . . ." Her voice trailed away.

"Mysterious?" suggested father.

"Yes, of course. Mysterious. But more than that. Dangerous."

"He's dangerous all right." Father said it in a musing way. Then he chuckled. "But not to us, my dear." And then he said what seemed to me a curious thing. "In fact, I don't think you ever had a safer man in your house."

Let Me Tell You about My Ma

Marinus Swets

My mother's eccentricities never hurt anyone; in fact, their consequences often were worthwhile in some way, like my recalling some of them now with what I feel as tenderness and affection. Living through them while we were children was not always agreeable to us; we often resisted complying with the immutable laws resulting through and from those eccentricities. There were minor skirmishes in our household because we kids or our pa resisted her laws.

I remember well many of these small hubbubs, which were, I am sure, different only in kind from hubbubs in households all along the middle-class blocks of the neighborhoods of our town. Remembering them, I get a warm glow within me. I am grieved that she and her days are gone, but I am happy that she was what she was, special and distinctive. Hence, the memories of her and her days are alive and strong.

Take the seasons, for example. Ma calculated the clothing we were to wear according to certain Dutch aphorisms. She never heard of a Beaufort Scale, and hearing of anything like it, she probably would have dispensed with it, using other calendar wisdom. Ma's aphorism for March was *Maart roert zijn staart.* That means, literally, *March stirs his tail.* Undependable cat, that March, so bundle up. We could moan, plead, rail against, holler, bawl, but no use. No matter how bright the prospects for the day—sunny, warm west wind, birds chirping—it was March to Ma. And March meant what it was, so off to school we were sent, attired like tramps leaving town wearing their entire wardrobe.

April was no better. You would think that with spring officially ten days old we would get a break and could dress accordingly. Nothing doing. The April Dutchism was *Aprilletje zoet geeft een witte hoed,* or, *Sweet little April gives a white hat.* That tells you that April will give you snow at any time during his tenure. A typical day started at around a quarter to nine as we left for school. Breakfast was a quiet affair of oatmeal and a boiled egg. When we were ready to leave, however, the action would begin. Sneaky, trying to get out without looking like cocoons in galoshes, we heard Ma's voice breaking our stealth: "Boys, put your rubbers on."

"Aw, Ma, it's nice out."

"And your hats."

"Ma, it's hot out. It's boiling; the sun's really hot."

"And your jackets."

"Ma, listen to the birds singing."

"And you better put on your mittens and button up good."

"Aw. Ma. . . ."

"*Aprilletje zoet geeft een witte hoed.* 'Tis April yet." And that settled it. The conditions of the day meant nothing to Ma. Her first concern was for us. That the day often turned out nice, as it had promised, wouldn't change her. Just as often her precautions were justified by a Michigan storm at noon. April to her was treachery, uncertainty, grippe, snow, mud: a reflection, you might say, of life itself, in a way. No one could reason her out of her stand.

May was a little better. The May saying was *In Mei leggen de vogeltjes een ei.* No weather in that one. It says that the little birds lay an egg in May. So we were allowed to doff selected items of outerwear—but never the hats or rubbers. The spring breeze carried the head

cold; and mud, Ma knew, was ubiquitous. If the sidewalks were dry, the paths that we traversed through the vacant lots on our way home most certainly were not.

I have never been able to work out the power of almanac wisdom upon my kids. I can hurl Dutch, Irish, German, or Yiddish truth about the weather at them as they are ready to leave for school in the A.M.; yet, off they go in sneakers and bowling shirts that they buy at the Goodwill store, looking as poor as the current mode demands that they look. Life sure isn't very exciting at off-to-school time in my household.

My Ma had another thing about work and its fruits. Only hard work bore good fruit in her metaphysic. Like the poet Housman, what Ma wrought she wrung in a weary land. That was often her best demeanor, looking sort of pooped from all that wringing. Especially after the wash.

With Ma the wash was both a guest and a ritual. She used the most difficult way to get the whitest wash. Ma's ingredients were scalding water and bars of American Family Soap—big, brown, rectangular bars wrapped in waxy paper that often stuck to the soap as it was unwrapped. (Ma saved American Family Soap coupons. Three hundred and you got a yellow saucer—or maybe a teacup for an extra hundred.) She washed in a wringer washer. Ma had only two washers during her married lifetime, both wringer types, except for one strange interlude with a Universal Spindry, probably the ancient precursor of the post-war Easy Spindry. She got rid of the spindry after it chased her around the basement twice.

That wasn't the real reason, however. She could defend herself quite well with her wash-stick, a stick she used to poke around in the scalding water to get the clothes from one tub into the other or to get them up so she could feed a corner into the wringer. The real reason was that she considered the spindry a deceiver. While it was true that she could see clear water depart in the spin process, she didn't trust what she saw. The clothes, she maintained, only strained out the dirt, which remained in them. A wringer she liked because it pressed the dirt out. That spinner only took the clothes for a merry-go-round-ride, and they collected all the dirt.

Ma preferred feeding the soapy wash from the washer through the wringer into a rinse, then out of the rinse into another, then back into another fresh water rinse, and so on until the very rinse water was drinking clean. The final batch came out of the wringer smashed flat, stiff even before the hanging. It was hard work, to be sure, but hard work was to Ma in itself one of the few virtues that man could attain. An automatic? Never. The devil's invention resulting in idle time that led to evils like reading movie magazines and listening to daytime radio serials. When Ma washed down in the basement with scalding water and brown soap dissolving, with the steam and fumes from her handfired boiler rising, and with her there poking around in the wash mixture with her stick, it looked like a vision from Blake.

Painting was another manifestation of the efficacy of work to Ma. No paint job was good unless toiled under pain. Painting the house, for example, carried with it certain necessary adjuncts. It required clothing like white, paint-stained coveralls; sweaty, red bandannas hauled out at regular intervals by the painters to wipe sticky hairlicks out of bleary eyes; and starched, cheese-cloth Martin Senour caps. There were essential physical qualities like flaking hands from too many rinses in lacquer thinner, raspy coughs from painters' colic, and brown teeth from snuff sucking.

The painters had to haul in gallons of Dutch Boy

White Lead, assorted cans of linseed oil, turps, Japan dryer, and other alchemy. They had to lug miscellaneous junk like long, heavy, paint-insulated wooden ladders with rungs split and accompanying scaffolding, all of which was deposited in the back yard under the box elder long before the paint job commenced and left long after it was completed.

Ma knew that good painters had habits like gasping in the heat under the eaves and that they cussed at the many exposed rafters on the overhang. Their exclamations of "House sure is bigger than it looks, sure is a fooler" gained from Ma a smile of appreciative assent which indicated that she felt she was getting her money's worth.

Ma's experience with painters was that painting was travail. She believed that painters died early of horrors of the liver and other organs. Ma's favorite painter always left his mark, blood-flecked driblets of phlegm that he spat here and there. He always dribbled a little of the phlegmy flecks from the corners of his mouth along with orts of Copenhagen. We could tell that he had mixed paints in our basement long after he had gone: he left his traces. That painter did, indeed, wring it in his weary land, suffering as he journeyed. Ma liked him. She knew quality when she saw it.

In the later years after the good painters all had departed, we undertook to paint her house for her. We came on anemically in Bermudas with some cans of rubber-base paint; a couple of lamb's wool rollers; one unblemished aluminum ladder; and, surreptitiously, a couple of six-packs. Neither we nor our attachment gear suited her. We should have been grimmer with other, grimmer paraphernalia. We looked like no sweat.

Her stern disapproval notwithstanding, we painted her house without a lunch break. A beer on a ladder is precarious but not impossible. Our near-sighs as we came to grimy terms with one eaves rafter after another we drowned in one swig of Bud after another. There were no coughs from the lead-anguish. We even painted in a light drizzle, singing in the rain. Our meager equipment was conspicuous only by how well we could conceal it under one bush as we left for the day.

The house looked great to us. Just like a Lucite ad. But if we were the Lucite boys, Ma was no Lucite girl. It all hadn't been oily or hot or dirty or treacly enough to Ma. We had been too happy during the job and not happy enough at getting it done. And no phlegm. Therefore, the house was not glory.

So we never felt completely at ease on summer evenings thereafter while visiting and looking over the petunias that we had planted in haste just before Mother's Day. As we were admiring them, Ma was sneaking looks at some roller-lap marks that roller painting inevitably leaves as practiced by amateurs at 4 P.M. after a few Buds. We might try to divert her gaze, remarking at how well the paint under the eaves had withstood peeling. She wouldn't hit us on the head. She would only partially sigh at how hard John VanderVan had worked that hot summer when he had painted the house and at how afterwards he had died of the lead-anguish. No lap marks with his big brush . . . and good oil paint . . . not a roller job . . . hard worker, that VanderVan . . . on to his reward. . . . We might admire the petunias harder. But they, too, had their faults, being planted late and in haste. Ma would recall the grand blooms of Holland. "But these look nice too, Ma," we would assure her.

"Maybe so," she would answer, "but next year I think that I will want impatiens here." The pun was not lost upon us.

Ma had a marvelous restraint. She never raised her voice, except sometimes when it all just got too much. Then she would send us to bed and maybe have a hassle with Pa. Pa never fought with anyone except in a somewhat furtive way, skirting the area and leaving his sign, so to speak, to worry you. Ma would get miffed periodically at Pa's stealing Sunday peppermints on Thursday, sneaking cookies on Sunday that were to have lasted all week, cutting chunks of white baloney (that was fresh liver sausage; a nickel's worth of white and a nickel's worth of red baloney at the meat market each Friday), sleeping in church, clicking against his teeth his glass or utensil when he put them to his mouth (a petty annoyance that bugged Ma), or other exasperating behaviors. Add to these his unexpiring optimism in the face of Ma's depression blues from trying to make a go of it on nothing and her personal miseries, which were many. Ma had to let it all go on selected Friday nights.

There weren't many better than Pa and Ma. They had something deep and abiding between them for the better part of three decades. The last years together, Ma tenderly cared for Pa as he diminished from arthritis and other maladies. I think that Ma and Pa were ahead of their times in their Friday night upheavals. They were engaging in two-man sensitivity sessions.

The battlefield, the kitchen, was Ma's choice, as were her weapons, American Family Soap coupon loot: faded yellow teacups and cracked plates and saucers. Pa didn't know that these were from the old sets; neither did we. The arguments usually started with words that soon became too weak to carry the weight of the frustrations. As the words became fewer, they also became less a vehicle to carry what either wanted to say. So Ma, as the apex of the evening approached, would vent a proper epithet like, "You know I can't stand it. If this keeps up, I'll fall off my stick."

She would follow that desperate statement with a teacup hurled over the kitchen table against the far wall where it would disintegrate into dust and slivers of clay. My brother Ade and I would pull the covers up and hide, not so much from terror as from good politics. To appear terrified was a good sign of respect.

One nice thing, Pa fought fair. Getting into the spirit of things, he would adopt Ma's tactics. As Ma shouted another soul-wracking invocation, like, "You know how long I've lived and where it's been and what it's like," tossing a yellow saucer into the sink and smashing it, Pa would follow with his own desperation: "Ya, you don't understand how sometimes my head feels weak, you know that?" And he would grab for a handy plate to heave it a ways. Then Ma: "No! No! Not that one. That's from the good set. Here, throw this one."

Thereupon, we would emerge from the blankets. Fight was over. No winner or loser. No make up. No love and kisses. Only going to bed feeling better, and Ma softly crying as she tucked us in again, telling us to be good boys.

These events and circumstances and others like them were the result of Ma's appraisal of what she termed "the realities of life." She wanted to be serious, setting for us a good example of the proper demeanor. She saw life's absurdities and didn't hesitate to share her vision. When she spoke of the realities it was, however, as though only she ever really experienced them. That was her tone. But the implication was there, that we, too, would one day be confronted by these realities.

As I get older, I gather more and more what she felt: a stiffening in the joints; the loss of a friend or relative; small and large hopes blown; future diminishing and past extending farther back; a dying universe, it seems; other griefs—and many more. To dwell upon them is poison for the soul. She knew that. Her eccentricities might have been planned to keep us limber in the course of stiffening realities that were inevitable. Maybe she didn't want us to become too impressed with her ostensible pessimism and stern visage.

On the other hand, I am not too sure of all that. Yet I do know that we had love at home, love and security, and then some. So much, in fact, that I can tell about Ma's qualities and not be afraid that anyone who knows me and knew her will come up to me and say that I shouldn't be telling these things about her. I get a warm glow just recalling her and her days. Sometimes I wish they were back.

A Mother in Mannville

Marjorie Kinnan Rawlings

Little did the woman in this story realize what her brief stay in the mountain cabin would mean to Jerry—the boy who chopped her firewood with such pride and care.

The orphanage is high in the Carolina mountains. Sometimes in winter the snowdrifts are so deep that the institution is cut off from the village below, from all the world. Fog hides the mountain peaks, the snow swirls down the valleys, and a wind blows so bitterly that the orphanage boys who take the milk twice daily to the baby cottage reach the door with fingers stiff in an agony of numbness.

"Or when we carry trays from the cookhouse for the ones that are sick," Jerry said, "we get our faces frost-bit, because we can't put our hands over them. I have gloves," he added. "Some of the boys don't have any."

He liked the late spring, he said. The rhododendron was in bloom, a carpet of color, across the mountain-sides, soft as the May winds that stirred the hemlocks. He called it laurel.

"It's pretty when the laurel blooms," he said. "Some of it's pink and some of it's white."

I was there in the autumn. I wanted quiet, isolation, to do some troublesome writing. I wanted mountain air to blow out the malaria from too long a time in the subtropics. I was homesick, too, for the flaming of maples in October, and for corn shocks and pumpkins and black-walnut trees and the lift of hills. I found them all, living in a cabin that belonged to the orphanage, half a mile beyond the orphanage farm. When I took the cabin, I asked for a boy or man to come and chop wood for the fireplace. The first few days were warm, and I found what wood I needed about the cabin; no one came, and I forgot the order.

I looked up from my typewriter one late afternoon, a little startled. A boy stood at the door, and my pointer dog, my companion, was at his side, and had not barked to warn me. The boy was probably twelve years old, but undersized. He wore overalls and a torn shirt, and was barefooted.

He said, "I can chop some wood today."

I said, "But I have a boy coming from the orphanage."

"I'm the boy."

"You? But you're small."

"Size don't matter, chopping wood," he said. "Some

of the big boys don't chop good. I've been chopping wood at the orphanage a long time."

I visualized mangled and inadequate branches for my fires. I was well into my work and not inclined to conversation. I was a little blunt.

"Very well. There's the ax. Go ahead and see what you can do."

I went back to work, closing the door. At first the sound of the boy dragging brush annoyed me. Then he began to chop. The blows were rhythmic and steady, and shortly I had forgotten him, the sound no more of an interruption than a consistent rain. I suppose an hour and a half passed, for when I stopped and stretched, and heard the boy's steps on the cabin stoop, the sun was dropping behind the farthest mountain, and the valleys were purple, with something deeper than asters.

The boy said, "I have to go to supper now. I can come again tomorrow evening."

I said, "I'll pay you now for what you've done," thinking I should probably have to insist on an older boy. "Ten cents an hour?"

"Anything is all right."

We went together back of the cabin. An astonishing amount of solid wood had been cut. There were cherry logs and heavy roots of rhododendron, and blocks from the waste pine and oak left from the building of the cabin.

"But you've done as much as a man," I said. "This is a splendid pile."

I looked at him, actually, for the first time. His hair was the color of the corn shocks and his eyes, very direct, were like the mountain sky when rain is pending–gray, with a shadowing of that miraculous blue. As I spoke, a light came over him, as though the setting sun had touched him with the same suffused glory with which it touched the mountains. I gave him a quarter.

"You may come tomorrow," I said, "and thank you very much."

He looked at me, and at the coin, and seemed to want to speak, but could not, and turned away.

"I'll split kindling tomorrow," he said over his thin ragged shoulder. "You'll need kindling and medium wood and logs and backlogs."

At daylight I was half wakened by the sound of chopping. Again it was so even in texture that I went back to sleep. When I left my bed in the cool morning, the boy had come and gone, and a stack of kindling was neat against the cabin wall. He came again after school in the afternoon and worked until time to return to the orphanage. His name was Jerry; he was twelve years old, and he had been at the orphanage since he was four. I could picture him at four, with the same grave gray-blue eyes and the same—independence? No, the word that comes to me is "integrity."

The word means something very special to me, and the quality for which I use it is a rare one. My father had it—there is another of whom I am almost sure—but almost no man of my acquaintance possesses it with the clarity, the purity, the simplicity of a mountain stream. But the boy Jerry had it. It is bedded on courage, but it is more than honesty. The ax handle broke one day. Jerry said the woodshop at the orphanage would repair it. I brought money to pay for the job and he refused it.

"I'll pay for it," he said. "I broke it. I brought the ax down careless."

"But no one hits accurately every time," I told him. "The fault was in the wood of the handle. I'll see the man from whom I bought it."

It was only then that he would take the money. He

was standing back of his own carelessness. He was a freewill agent and he chose to do careful work, and if he failed, he took the responsibility without subterfuge.

And he did for me the unnecessary thing, the gracious thing, that we find done only by the great of heart. Things no training can teach, for they are done on the instant, with no predicated experience. He found a cubbyhole beside the fireplace that I had not noticed. There, of his own accord, he put kindling and "medium" wood, so that I might always have dry fire material ready in case of sudden wet weather. A stone was loose in the rough walk to the cabin. He dug a deeper hole and steadied it, although he came, himself, by a short cut over the bank. I found that when I tried to return his thoughtfulness with such things as candy and apples, he was wordless. "Thank you" was, perhaps, an expression for which he had no use, for his courtesy was instinctive. He only looked at the gift and at me, and a curtain lifted, so that I saw deep into the clear well of his eyes, and gratitude was there, and affection, soft over the firm granite of his character.

He made simple excuses to come and sit with me. I could no more have turned him away than if he had been physically hungry. I suggested once that the best time for us to visit was just before supper, when I left off my writing. After that, he waited always until my typewriter had been some time quiet. One day I worked until nearly dark. I went outside the cabin, having forgotten him. I saw him going up over the hill in the twilight toward the orphanage. When I sat down on my stoop, a place was warm from his body where he had been sitting.

He became intimate, of course, with my pointer, Pat. There is a strange communication between a boy and a dog. Perhaps they possess the same singleness of spirit, the same kind of wisdom. It is difficult to explain, but it exists. When I went across the state for a weekend, I left the dog in Jerry's charge. I gave him the dog whistle and the key to the cabin, and left sufficient food. He was to come two or three times a day and let out the dog, and feed and exercise him. I should return Sunday night, and Jerry would take out the dog for the last time Sunday afternoon and then leave the key under an agreed hiding place.

My return was belated and fog filled the mountain passes so treacherously that I dared not drive at night. The fog held the next morning, and it was Monday noon before I reached the cabin. The dog had been fed and cared for that morning. Jerry came early in the afternoon, anxious.

"The superintendent said nobody would drive in the fog," he said. "I came just before bedtime last night and you hadn't come. So I brought Pat some of my breakfast this morning. I wouldn't have let anything happen to him."

"I was sure of that. I didn't worry."

"When I heard about the fog, I thought you'd know."

He was needed for work at the orphanage and he had to return at once. I gave him a dollar in payment, and he looked at it and went away. But that night he came in the darkness and knocked at the door.

"Come in, Jerry," I said, "if you're allowed to be away this late."

"I told maybe a story," he said. "I told them I thought you would want to see me."

"That's true," I assured him, and I saw his relief. "I want to hear about how you managed with the dog."

He sat by the fire with me, with no other light, and told me of their two days together. The dog lay close to him, and found a comfort there that I did not have for him. And it seemed to me that being with my dog, and caring for him, had brought the boy and me, too, together, so that he felt that he belonged to me as well as to the animal.

"He stayed right with me," he told me, "except when he ran in the laurel. He likes the laurel. I took him up over the hill and we both ran fast. There was a place where the grass was high and I lay down in it and hid. I could hear Pat hunting for me. He found my trail and he barked. When he found me, he acted crazy, and he ran around and around me, in circles."

We watched the flames.

"That's an apple log," he said. "It burns the prettiest of any wood."

We were very close.

He was suddenly impelled to speak of things he had not spoken of before, nor had I cared to ask him.

"You look a little bit like my mother," he said. "Especially in the dark, by the fire."

"But you were only four, Jerry, when you came here. You have remembered how she looked, all these years?"

"My mother lives in Mannville," he said.

For a moment, finding that he had a mother shocked me as greatly as anything in my life has ever done, and I did not know why it disturbed me. Then I understood my distress. I was filled with a passionate resentment that any woman should go away and leave her son. A fresh anger added itself. A son like this one—. The orphanage was a wholesome place, the executives were kind, good people, the food was more than adequate, the boys were healthy, a ragged shirt was no hardship, nor the doing of clean labor. Granted, perhaps, that the boy felt no lack, but what mother would not yearn over the body of this child, her own? At four he would have looked the same as now. Nothing, I thought, nothing in life could change those eyes. His quality must be apparent to an idiot, a fool. I burned with questions I could not ask. In any, I was afraid, there would be pain.

"Have you seen her, Jerry—lately?"

"I see her every summer. She sends for me."

I wanted to cry out, "Why are you not with her? How can she let you go away again?"

He said, "She comes up here from Mannville whenever she can. She doesn't have a job now."

His face shone in the firelight.

"She wanted to give me a puppy, but they can't let any one boy keep a puppy. You remember the suit I had on last Sunday?" He was plainly proud. "She sent me that for Christmas. The Christmas before that"—he drew a long breath, savoring the memory—"she sent me a pair of skates."

"Roller skates?"

My mind was busy, making pictures of her, trying to understand her. She had not, then, entirely deserted or forgotten him. But why, then—I thought, "I must not condemn her without knowing."

"Roller skates. I let the other boys use them. They're always borrowing them. But they're careful of them."

What circumstances other than poverty—

"I'm going to take the dollar you gave me for taking care of Pat," he said, "and buy her a pair of gloves."

I could only say, "That will be nice. Do you know her size?"

"I think it's 8½," he said.

He looked at my hands.

"Do you wear 8½?" he asked.

"No. I wear a smaller size, a 6."

"Oh! Then I guess her hands are bigger than yours."

I hated her. Poverty or no, there was other food than bread, and the soul could starve as quickly as the body.

He was taking his dollar to buy gloves for her big stupid hands, and she lived away from him, in Mannville, and contented herself with sending him skates.

"She likes white gloves," he said. "Do you think I can get them for a dollar?"

"I think so," I said.

I decided that I should not leave the mountains without seeing her and knowing for myself why she had done this thing.

The human mind scatters its interests as though made of thistledown, and every wind stirs and moves it. I finished my work. It did not please me, and I gave my thoughts to another field. I should need some Mexican material.

I made arrangements to close my Florida place. Mexico immediately, and doing the writing there, if conditions were favorable. Then, Alaska with my brother. After that, who could tell what or where?

I did not take time to go to Mannville to see Jerry's mother, nor even to talk with the orphanage officials about her. I was a trifle abstracted about the boy, because of my work and plans. And after my first fury at her—we did not speak of her again—his having a mother, any sort at all, not far away, in Mannville, relieved me of the ache I had had about him. He did not question the anomalous relation. He was not lonely. It was none of my concern.

He came every day and cut my wood and did small helpful favors and stayed to talk. The days had become cold, and often I let him come inside the cabin. He would lie on the floor in front of the fire, with one arm across the pointer, and they would both doze and wait quietly for me. Other days they ran with a common ecstasy through the laurel, and since the asters were now gone, he brought me back vermilion maple leaves, and chestnut boughs dripping with imperial yellow. I was ready to go.

I said to him, "You have been my good friend, Jerry. I shall often think of you and miss you. Pat will miss you too. I am leaving tomorrow."

He did not answer. When he went away, I remembered that a new moon hung over the mountains and I watched him go in silence up the hill. I expected him the next day, but he did not come. The details of packing my personal belongings, loading my car, arranging the bed over the seat, where the dog would ride, occupied me until late in the day. I closed the cabin and started the car, noticing that the sun was in the west and I should do well to be out of the mountains by nightfall. I stopped by the orphanage and left the cabin key and money for my light bill with Miss Clark.

"And will you call Jerry for me to say good-by to him?"

"I don't know where he is," she said. "I'm afraid he's not well. He didn't eat his dinner this noon. One of the other boys saw him going over the hill into the laurel. He was supposed to fire the boiler this afternoon. It's not like him: he's unusually reliable."

I was almost relieved, for I knew I should never see him again, and it would be easier not to say good-by to him.

I said, "I wanted to talk with you about his mother—why he's here—but I'm in more of a hurry than I expected to be. It's out of the question for me to see her now too. But here's some money I'd like to leave with you to buy things for him at Christmas and on his birthday. It will be better than for me to try to send him things. I could so easily duplicate—skates, for instance."

She blinked her honest eyes.

"There's not much use for skates here," she said.

Her stupidity annoyed me.

"What I mean," I said, "is that I don't want to duplicate things his mother sends him. I might have chosen skates if I didn't know she had already given them to him."

She stared at me.

"I don't understand," she said. "He has no mother. He has no skates."

Sunday Morning

Why does the doxology always
   have to be pitched so high?
   We pay the organist enough. He should
   know better. Why—
   there are the Winters'. They haven't
   been out in months. I'm amazed they'll
   show their faces, even now—
   the rumors I've heard!
Now a psalm is being read. It is a
   long psalm. David got
   rather emotional at times.
   Exaggerated, surely? No sense of perspective.
   No *restraint.*
   I see they've put in the stained glass at last.
   Very effective, that combination
   of rose and purple.

Ah, the pastoral prayer.
  We cross our knees the other way.
  Warm, isn't it?
Eyes earnestly closed now . . .
  Someone may notice our sincerity.
  All the other heads are nodding
  at the right angle.
  Hands piously postured. Amens
  intoned with just the right proportion
  of reverence and fervor.
The Offertory, and the clink of change. Don't
  tell me! I forgot my check!
And now the Sermon. *Sanctity*
  and Twentieth Century Society.
  Stimulating I hope. Sanctity is *so* necessary.
  I must talk to Pastor about this
  red plush. It's wearing thin.

At last—the Benediction.
  Well, he went overtime, as usual. My leg
  has gone to sleep.
  Hat on straight? Friendly now—
  "Oh, Mrs. Winters. Delightful to see you again!
  The prayer and missionary meeting?
  Yes, Tuesday. It *will* be a relief to get out-
  side, won't it? So stuffy
  in here."

Luci Shaw

Royalty

He was a plain man
and learned no latin

Having left all gold behind
he dealt out peace
to all us wild men
and the weather

He ate fish, bread,
country wine and God's will

Dust sandalled his feet

He wore purple only once
and that was an irony

Luci Shaw

Whose epitaph do you think this is?

Would you want it to be yours?

Irony is created when a result is opposite to and a mockery of what was expected. Do you see ironies in this poem?

Foul Shot

With two 60's stuck on the scoreboard
And two seconds hanging on the clock,
The solemn boy in the center of eyes,
Squeezed by silence,
Seeks out the line with his feet,
Soothes his hands along his uniform,
Gently drums the ball against the floor,
Then measures the waiting net,
Raises the ball on his right hand,
Balances it with his left,
Calms it with fingertips,
Breathes,
Crouches,
Waits,
And then through a stretching of stillness,
Nudges it upward.

The ball
Slides up and out,
Lands,
Leans,
Wobbles,
Wavers,
Hesitates,
Exasperates,
Plays it coy
Until every face begs with unsounding screams—
And then
                    And then
                                        And then

Right before ROAR-UP,
Drives down and through.

Edwin A. Hoey

The Base Stealer

Poised between going on and back, pulled
Both ways taut like a tightrope-walker,
Fingertips pointing the opposites,
Now bouncing tiptoe like a dropped ball
Or a kid skipping rope, come on, come on.
Running a scattering of steps sidewise,
How he teeters, skitters, tingles, teases,
Taunts them, hovers like an ecstatic bird,
He's only flirting, crowd him, crowd him,
Delicate, delicate, delicate, delicate—now!

Robert Francis

To Look at Any Thing

To look at any thing,
If you would know that thing,
You must look at it long:
To look at this green and say
"I have seen spring in these
Woods," will not do—you must
Be the thing you see:
You must be the dark snakes of
Stems and ferny plumes of leaves,
You must enter in
To the small silences between
The leaves,
You must take your time
And touch the very peace
They issue from.

John Moffitt

What are the elements or parts in the process that the poet describes? List the things you've "looked" at. Are you satisfied with your list? Does it matter whether your list is long or short?

Reflection

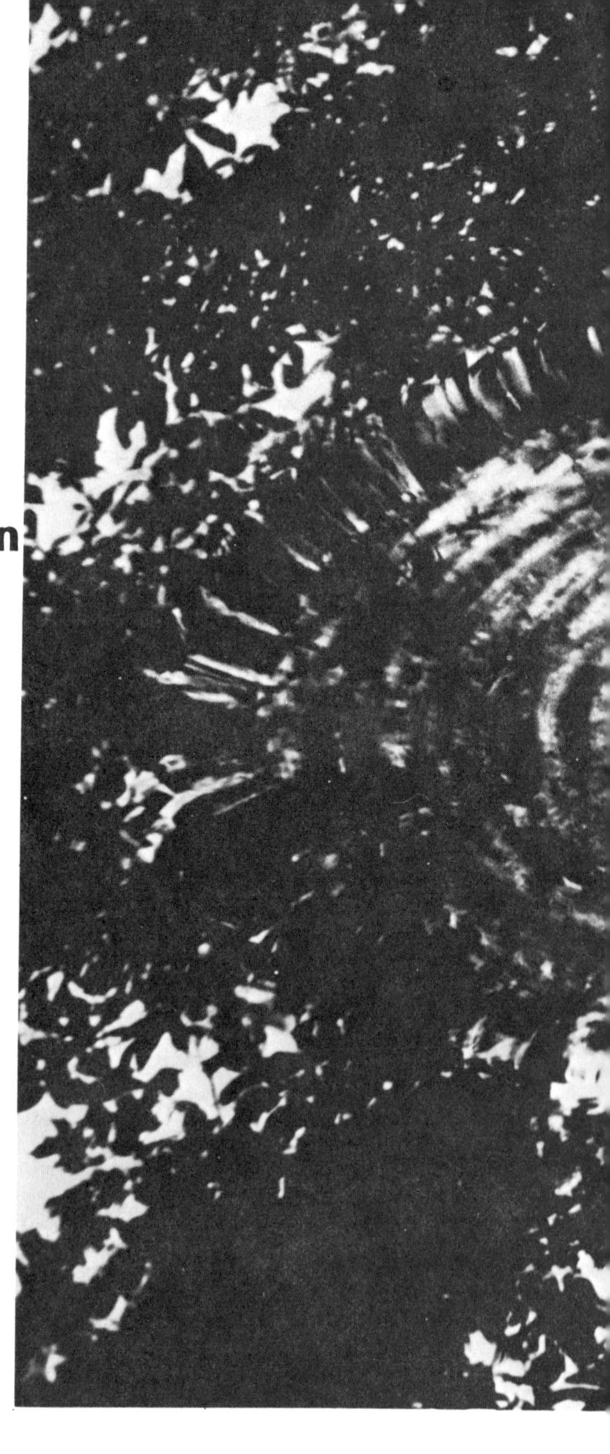

The Meadow Mouse

1

In a shoe box stuffed in an old nylon stocking
Sleeps the baby mouse I found in the meadow,
Where he trembled and shook beneath a stick
Till I caught him up by the tail and brought him in,
Cradled in my hand,
A little quaker, the whole body of him trembling,
His absurd whiskers sticking out like a cartoon-mouse,
His feet like small leaves,
Little lizard-feet,
Whitish and spread wide when he tried to struggle away,
Wriggling like a miniscule puppy.

Now he's eaten his three kinds of cheese and drunk
from his bottle-cap watering-trough—
So much he just lies in one corner,
His tail curled under him, his belly big
As his head; his bat-like ears
Twitching, tilting toward the least sound.

Do I imagine he no longer trembles
When I come close to him?
He seems no longer to tremble.

2

But this morning the shoe-box house on the back porch
is empty.
Where has he gone, my meadow mouse,
My thumb of a child that nuzzled in my palm?—
To run under the hawk's wing,
Under the eye of the great owl watching from the
elm-tree,

To live by courtesy of the shrike, the snake, the tom-cat.

I think of the nestling fallen into the deep grass,
The turtle gasping in the dusty rubble of the highway,
The paralytic stunned in the tub, and the water rising,—
All things innocent, hapless, forsaken.

Theodore Roethke

To a Mouse

On Turning Her Up in Her Nest
with the Plow, November, 1785

The poem is written in Scottish dialect, the native speech of the poet.

Wee, sleekit,° cowrin', tim'rous beastie,
O, what a panic's in thy breastie!
Thou need na start awa sae hasty
Wi' bickering brattle!°
I wad be laith° to rin an' chase thee
Wi' murd'rin pattle!°

I'm truly sorry man's dominion
Has broken nature's social union,
And justifies that ill opinion
Which makes thee startle
At me, thy poor, earthborn companion,
An' fellow mortal!

1. *sleekit:* sleek. 4. *bickering brattle:* hasty scamper. 5. *laith* (lāth): loath, reluctant. 6. *pattle:* plowstaff.

I doubt na, whyles,° but thou may
thieve;
What then? poor beastie, thou maun
live!
A daimen icker in a thrave°
'S a sma' request;
I'll get a blessin' wi' the lave,°
An' never miss 't!

Thy wee bit housie, too, in ruin!
It's silly wa's° the win's are strewin'!
An' naething, now, to big a new ane,°
O' foggage° green!
An' bleak December's winds ensuin',
Baith snell° an' keen!

Thou saw the fields laid bare and waste,
An' weary winter comin' fast,
An' cozie here, beneath the blast,
Thou thought to dwell,
Till crash! the cruel coulter° passed
Out through thy cell.

That wee bit heap o' leaves an' stibble
Has cost thee mony a weary nibble!
Now thou's turn'd out, for a' thy trouble,
But house or hald,°

13. *whyles:* at times. 15. *A daimen . . . thrave*: an occasional head of grain in a shock. 17. *lave:* rest. 20. *silly wa's*: weak walls. 21. *big . . . ane*: build a new one. 22. *foggage*: herbage. 24. *snell*: sharp. 29. *coulter* (kōl′ tẽr): plow. 34. *But house or hald*: without a dwelling place.

To thole° the winter's sleety dribble
An' cranreuch° cauld!

But, Mousie, thou art no thy lane°
In proving foresight may be vain;
The best laid schemes o' mice an' men
Gang aft agley,°
An' lea'e us nought but grief an' pain,
For promis'd joy.

Still thou art blest, compared wi' me,
The present only toucheth thee;
But och! I backward cast my e'e
On prospects drear!
An' forward, though I canna see,
I guess an' fear!

Robert Burns

35. *thole*: endure. 36. *cranreuch* (krån′ rŭk): hoarfrost. 37. *no thy lane*: not alone. 40. *Gang aft agley* (å glē′): oft go astray.

A Narrow Fellow in the Grass

A narrow fellow in the grass
Occasionally rides;
You may have met him,—did you not?
His notice sudden is.

The grass divides as with a comb,
A spotted shaft is seen;
And then it closes at your feet
And opens further on.

He likes a boggy acre,
A floor too cool for corn.
Yet when a child, and barefoot,
I more than once, at morn,

Have passed, I thought, a whip-lash
Unbraiding in the sun,—
When, stooping to secure it,
It wrinkled, and was gone.

Several of nature's people
I know, and they know me;
I feel for them a transport
Of cordiality;

But never met this fellow,
Attended or alone,
Without a tighter breathing,
And zero at the bone.

Emily Dickinson

What experiences have you had that produced an effect similar to the one described in this poem?

What possible second "level" of meaning would occur if you interpret the garden, the snake, and the child as symbolic?

Traveling through the Dark

Traveling through the dark I found a deer
dead on the edge of the Wilson River road.
It is usually best to roll them into the canyon:
that road is narrow; to swerve might make more dead.

By glow of the tail-light I stumbled back of the car
and stood by the heap, a doe, a recent killing;
she had stiffened already, almost cold.
I dragged her off; she was large in the belly.

My fingers touching her side brought me the reason—
her side was warm; her fawn lay there waiting,
alive, still, never to be born.
Beside that mountain road I hesitated.

The car aimed ahead its lowered parking lights;
under the hood purred the steady engine.
I stood in the glare of the warm exhaust turning red;
around our group I could hear the wilderness listen.

I thought hard for us all—my only swerving—
then pushed her over the edge into the river.

William Stafford

Interlude III

Writing, I crushed an insect with my nail
And thought nothing at all. A bit of wing
Caught my eye then, a gossamer so frail

And exquisite, I saw in it a thing
That scorned the grossness of the thing I wrote.
It hung upon my finger like a sting.

A leg I noticed next, fine as a mote,
"And on this frail eyelash he walked," I said.
"And climbed and walked like any mountain-goat."

And in this mood I sought the little head,
But it was lost; then in my heart a fear
Cried out, "A life—why, beautiful, why dead!"

It was a mite that held itself most dear,
So small I could have drowned it with a tear.

Karl Shapiro

What is the discovery the poet makes here? How is this poem like "Traveling through the Dark" and the following poem, "On a Squirrel Crossing the Road in Autumn, in New England"?

On a Squirrel Crossing the Road in Autumn, in New England

It is what he does not know,
Crossing the road under the elm trees,
About the mechanism of my car,
About the Commonwealth of Massachusetts,
About Mozart, India, Arcturus,

That wins my praise. I engage
At once in whirling squirrel-praise.
He obeys the orders of nature
Without knowing them.
It is what he does not know
That makes him beautiful.
Such a knot of little purposeful nature!

I who can see him as he cannot see himself
Repose in the ignorance that is his blessing.

It is what man does not know of God
Composes the visible poem of the world.

. . . Just missed him!

Richard Eberhart

Why does the speaker praise the squirrel's ignorance? Does the speaker also say to man that "ignorance is bliss"?

What possible conflict do you perceive between the thrust of this poem and "To Look at Any Thing"?

On Watching the Construction of a Skyscraper

Nothing sings from these orange trees,
Rindless steel as smooth as sapling skin,
Except a crane's brief wheeze
And all the muffled, clanking din
Of rivets nosing in like bees.

Burton Raffel

Southbound on the Freeway

A tourist came in from Orbitville,
parked in the air, and said:

The creatures of this star
are made of metal and glass.

Through the transparent parts
you can see their guts.

Their feet are round and roll
on diagrams or long

measuring tapes, dark
with white lines.

They have four eyes.
The two in back are red.

Sometimes you can see a five-eyed
one, with a red eye turning

on the top of his head.
He must be special—

the others respect him
and go slow

when he passes, winding
among them from behind.

They all hiss as they glide,
like inches, down the marked

tapes. Those soft shapes,
shadowy inside

the hard bodies—are they
their guts or their brains?

May Swenson

Rural Dumpheap

This rusty mound of cans,
This scatter of tires and pans,
This litter of mattresses and twisted springs,
This rotting refuse, these abandoned things
Malodorously flung,—this impudent pile
That dares to choke the current, to defile
The innocent season,—all are man's.

Man's inhumanity to sod
Makes countless snowdrops mourn,
And every gentle seed that's born
Gives battle for a dishonored god.

Within the heap and darkly, heaves
The growing mutiny of leaves,
While down the valley bird to bird
Relays the rallying word,
And courage calls on every breeze
To armies of anemones,
And triumph scales the parapet,
A host of violet.

O man, where is thy victory?
Despite this blight of tins,
The fern persists and cleaves and wins,
And, gladly, spring begins.

Melville Cane

Chameleon Finds

retold by Maria Leach

This myth is told by the Yao people who live in northern Mozambique in Africa.

At first there were no people. Only Mulungu and the decent peaceful beasts were in the world.

One day Chameleon sat weaving a fish trap, and when he had finished he set it in the river. In the morning he pulled the trap and it was full of fish, which he took home and ate.

He set the trap again. In the morning he pulled it out and it was empty: no fish.

"Bad luck," he said, and set the trap again.

The next morning when he pulled the trap he found a little man and woman in it. He had never seen any creatures like this.

"What can they be?" he said. "Today I behold the unknown." And he picked up the fish trap and took the two creatures to Mulungu.

"Father," said Chameleon, "see what I have brought."

Mulungu looked. "Take them out of the trap," he said. "Put them down on the earth and they will grow."

Chameleon did this. And the man and woman grew. They grew until they became as tall as men and women are today.

All the animals watched to see what the people would do. They made fire. They rubbed two sticks together in a special way and thus made fire. The fire caught in the bush and roared through the forest and the animals had to run to escape the flames.

The people caught a buffalo and killed it and roasted it in the fire and ate it. Then next day they did the same thing. Every day they set fires and killed some animal and ate it.

"They are burning up everything!" said Mulungu. "They are killing my people!"

All the beasts ran into the forest as far away from mankind as they could get. Chameleon went into the high trees.

"I'm leaving!" said Mulungu.

He called to Spider. "How do you climb on high?" he said.

"Very nicely," said Spider. And Spider spun a rope for Mulungu and Mulungu climbed the rope and went to live in the sky.

Thus the gods were driven off the face of the earth by the cruelty of man.

Do you agree that man is the way this myth illustrates?

Virtuoso

Herbert Goldstone

"Sir?"

The Maestro continued to play, not looking up from the keys.

"Yes, Rollo?"

"Sir, I was wondering if you would explain this apparatus to me."

The Maestro stopped playing, his thin body stiffly relaxed on the bench. His long supple fingers floated off the keyboard.

"Apparatus?" He turned and smiled at the robot. "Do you mean the piano, Rollo?"

"This machine that produces varying sounds. I would like some information about it, its operation and purpose. It is not included in my reference data."

The Maestro lit a cigarette. He preferred to do it himself. One of his first orders to Rollo when the robot was delivered two days before had been to disregard his built-in instructions on the subject.

"I'd hardly call a piano a machine, Rollo," he smiled, "although technically you are correct. It is actually, I suppose, a machine designed to produce sounds of graduated pitch and tone, singly or in groups."

"I assimilated that much by observation," Rollo replied in a brassy baritone which no longer sent tiny tremors up the Maestro's spine. "Wires of different thickness and tautness struck by felt-covered hammers activated by manually operated levers arranged in a horizontal panel."

"A very cold-blooded description of one of man's nobler works," the Maestro remarked dryly. "You make Mozart and Chopin mere laboratory technicians."

"Mozart? Chopin?" The duralloy sphere that was Rollo's head shone stark and featureless, its immediate surface unbroken but for twin vision lenses. "The terms are not included in my memory banks."

"No, not yours, Rollo," the Maestro said softly. "Mozart and Chopin are not for vacuum tubes and fuses and copper wire. They are for flesh and blood and human tears."

"I do not understand," Rollo droned.

"Well," the Maestro said, smoke curling lazily from his nostrils, "they are two of the humans who compose, or design successions of notes—varying sounds, that is, produced by the piano or by other instruments, machines that produce other types of sounds of fixed pitch and tone.

"Sometimes these instruments, as we call them, are played, or operated, individually; sometimes in groups—orchestras, as we refer to them—and the sounds blend together, they harmonize. That is, they have an orderly, mathematical relationship to each other which results in . . ."

The Maestro threw up his hands.

"I never imagined," he chuckled, "that I would some day struggle so mightily, and so futilely, to explain music to a robot!"

"Music?"

"Yes, Rollo. The sounds produced by this machine and others of the same category are called music."

"What is the purpose of music, sir?"

"Purpose?"

The Maestro crushed the cigarette in an ash tray. He turned to the keyboard of the concert grand and flexed his fingers briefly.

"Listen, Rollo."

The wraithlike fingers glided and wove the opening

bars of "Clair de Lune," slender and delicate as spider silk. Rollo stood rigid, the fluorescent light over the music rack casting a bluish jeweled sheen over his towering bulk, shimmering in the amber vision lenses.

The Maestro drew his hands back from the keys and the subtle thread of melody melted reluctantly into silence.

"Claude Debussy," the Maestro said. "One of our mechanics of an era long past. He designed that succession of tones many years ago. What do you think of it?"

Rollo did not answer at once.

"The sounds were well formed," he replied finally. "They did not jar my auditory senses as some do."

The Maestro laughed. "Rollo, you may not realize it, but you're a wonderful critic."

"This music, then," Rollo droned. "Its purpose is to give pleasure to humans?"

"Exactly," the Maestro said. "Sounds well formed, that do not jar the auditory senses as some do. Marvelous! It should be carved in marble over the entrance of New Carnegie Hall."

"I do not understand. Why should my definition–?"

The Maestro waved a hand. "No matter, Rollo. No matter."

"Sir?"

"Yes, Rollo?"

"Those sheets of paper you sometimes place before you on the piano. They are the plans of the composer indicating which sounds are to be produced by the piano and in what order?"

"Just so. We call each sound a note; combinations of notes we call chords."

"Each dot, then, indicates a sound to be made?"

"Perfectly correct, my man of metal."

Rollo stared straight ahead. The Maestro felt a peculiar sense of wheels turning within that impregnable sphere.

"Sir, I have scanned my memory banks and find no specific or implied instructions against it. I should like to be taught how to produce these notes on the piano. I request that you feed the correlation between those dots and the levers of the panel into my memory banks."

The Maestro peered at him, amazed. A slow grin traveled across his face.

"Done!" he exclaimed. "It's been many years since pupils helped gray these ancient locks, but I have the feeling that you, Rollo, will prove a most fascinating student. To instill the Muse into metal and machinery . . . I accept the challenge gladly!"

He rose, touched the cool latent power of Rollo's arm.

"Sit down here, my Rolleindex Personal Robot, Model M-e. We shall start Beethoven spinning in his grave—or make musical history."

More than an hour later the Maestro yawned and looked at his watch.

"It's late," he spoke into the end of the yawn. "These old eyes are not tireless like yours, my friend." He touched Rollo's shoulder. "You have the complete fundamentals of musical notation in your memory banks, Rollo. That's a good night's lesson, particularly when I recall how long it took me to acquire the same amount of information. Tomorrow we'll attempt to put those awesome fingers of yours to work."

He stretched. "I'm going to bed," he said. "Will you lock up and put out the lights?"

Rollo rose from the bench. "Yes, sir," he droned. "I have a request."

"What can I do for my star pupil?"

"May I attempt to create some sounds with the keyboard tonight? I will do so very softly so as not to disturb you."

"Tonight? Aren't you–?" Then the Maestro smiled. "You must pardon me, Rollo. It's still a bit difficult for me to realize that sleep has no meaning for you."

He hesitated, rubbing his chin. "Well, I suppose a good teacher should not discourage impatience to learn. All right, Rollo, but please be careful." He patted the polished mahogany. "This piano and I have been together for many years. I'd hate to see its teeth knocked out by those sledgehammer digits of yours. Lightly, my friend, very lightly."

"Yes, sir."

The Maestro fell asleep with a faint smile on his lips, dimly aware of the shy, tentative notes that Rollo was coaxing forth.

Then gray fog closed in and he was in that half-world where reality is dreamlike and dreams are real. It was soft and feathery and lavender clouds and sounds were rolling and washing across his mind in flowing waves.

Where? The mist drew back a bit and he was in red velvet and deep and the music swelled and broke over him.

He smiled.

My recording. Thank you, thank you, thank–

The Maestro snapped erect, threw the covers aside.

He sat on the edge of the bed, listening.

He groped for his robe in the darkness, shoved bony feet into his slippers.

He crept, trembling uncontrollably, to the door of his studio and stood there, thin and brittle in the robe.

The light over the music rack was an eerie island in the brown shadows of the studio. Rollo sat at the keyboard, prim, inhuman, rigid, twin lenses focused somewhere off into the shadows.

The massive feet working the pedals, arms and hands flashing and glinting—they were living entities, separate, somehow, from the machined perfection of his body.

The music rack was empty.

A copy of Beethoven's "Appassionata" lay closed on the bench. It had been, the Maestro remembered, in a pile of sheet music on the piano.

Rollo was playing it.

He was creating it, breathing it, drawing it through silver flame.

Time became meaningless, suspended in midair.

The Maestro didn't realize he was weeping until Rollo finished the sonata.

The robot turned to look at the Maestro. "The sounds," he droned. "They pleased you?"

The Maestro's lips quivered. "Yes, Rollo," he replied at last. "They pleased me." He fought the lump in his throat.

He picked up the music in fingers that shook.

"This," he murmured. "Already?"

"It has been added to my store of data," Rollo replied. "I applied the principles you explained to me to these plans. It was not very difficult."

The Maestro swallowed as he tried to speak. "It was not very difficult . . . " he repeated softly.

The old man sank down slowly onto the bench next to Rollo, stared silently at the robot as though seeing him for the first time.

Rollo got to his feet.

The Maestro let his fingers rest on the keys, strangely foreign now.

"Music!" he breathed. "I may have heard it that way in my soul. I know Beethoven did!"

He looked up at the robot, a growing excitement in his face.

"Rollo," he said, his voice straining to remain calm. "You and I have some work to do tomorrow on your memory banks."

Sleep did not come again that night.

He strode briskly into the studio the next morning. Rollo was vacuuming the carpet. The Maestro preferred carpets to the new dust-free plastics, which felt somehow profane to his feet.

The Maestro's house was, in fact, an oasis of anachronisms in a desert of contemporary antiseptic efficiency.

"Well, are you ready for work, Rollo?" he asked. "We have a lot to do, you and I. I have such plans for you, Rollo—great plans!"

Rollo, for once, did not reply.

"I have asked them all to come here this afternoon," the Maestro went on. "Conductors, concert pianists, composers, my manager. All the giants of music, Rollo. Wait until they hear you play."

Rollo switched off the vacuum and stood quietly.

"You'll play for them right here this afternoon." The Maestro's voice was high-pitched, breathless. "The 'Appassionata' again, I think. Yes, that's it. I must see their faces!

"Then we'll arrange a recital to introduce you to the public and the critics and then a major concerto with one of the big orchestras. We'll have it telecast around the world, Rollo. It can be arranged.

"Think of it, Rollo, just think of it! The greatest piano virtuoso of all time . . . a robot! It's completely fantastic and completely wonderful. I feel like an explorer at the edge of a new world."

He walked feverishly back and forth.

"Then recordings, of course. My entire repertoire, Rollo, and more. So much more!"

"Sir?"

The Maestro's face shone as he looked up at him. "Yes, Rollo?"

"In my built-in instructions, I have the option of rejecting any action which I consider harmful to my owner," the robot's words were precise, carefully selected. "Last night you wept. That is one of the indications I am instructed to consider in making my decisions."

The Maestro gripped Rollo's thick, superbly molded arm.

"Rollo, you don't understand. That was for the moment. It was petty of me, childish!"

"I beg your pardon, sir, but I must refuse to approach the piano again."

The Maestro stared at him, unbelieving, pleading.

"Rollo, you can't! The world must hear you!"

"No, sir." The amber lenses almost seemed to soften.

"The piano is not a machine," that powerful inhuman voice droned. "To me, yes. I can translate the notes into sounds at a glance. From only a few I am able to grasp at once the composer's conception. It is easy for me."

Rollo towered magnificently over the Maestro's bent form.

"I can also grasp," the brassy monotone rolled through the studio, "that this . . . music is not for robots. It is for man. To me it is easy, yes. . . . It was not meant to be easy."

What did the robot's "built-in instructions" fail to take into account about human experiences that produce tears?

Antaeus

retold by Dan Vander Ark

Hercules was now finished with his labors. Long before he had murdered his wife and three daughters in a mad rage. For that vicious deed, Hercules, the son of Zeus, the strongest man in all of Greece, felt sorry; as his guilt deepened, he went to the oracle to find out what the gods wanted him to do to atone for this terrible mad deed.

The oracle sent him to King Eurystheus, who told Hercules that he must do twelve labors, a series of penances, in order to relieve his guilt. Hercules began his difficult and dangerous labors by choking the life out of the Nemean lion which no weapon could wound. Each labor became more strenuous and daring as Hercules killed the nine-headed Hydra, captured a great boar, fetched a savage bull, retrieved the man-eating mares of Diomedes, brought back the Golden Apples of the Hesperides, and performed many other similarly daring deeds.

Now the twelfth and last labor was over. Hercules had brought the three-headed dog, Cerberus, up from Hades and back again. He had completed all the penances for killing his family and was on the way home. But just as he neared home, he passed the horrible house of Antaeus. Antaeus was a huge giant and mighty wrestler, who had been building for years a huge temple, roofed with human skulls.

Hercules was tired and relieved after all his labors, and was longing to live in ease and peace for the rest of his days. But that was not to be. Antaeus saw Hercules walking up the road. He had heard of the mighty Hercules and was jealously waiting to prove that he, Antaeus, was the greatest hero in all of Greece.

As Hercules came closer, Antaeus waited in a large clump of trees beside the road, ready to spring out at Hercules at just the right moment. Antaeus had been able to roof his temple with human skulls because he had challenged all his victims to wrestling matches with the stipulation that if he was victor, he should kill them. Just as Hercules came to a dense part of the woods, Antaeus pounced out in the road, throwing Hercules to the ground, screaming at the top of his thunderous voice, "Hercules, you are no hero! No one is stronger than I, Antaeus, the one who has killed enough men to roof a temple. You don't dare wrestle me, Hercules."

With that taunting boast ringing in his ears, Hercules grabbed Antaeus by his mangy hair and flung him to the ground.

"Antaeus, you shall not live. No man shall live who attacks Hercules." And with that the battle was on.

Antaeus fought hard, clawing at Hercules' eyes, kicking his stomach, and stomping on him whenever Hercules hit the ground. But Hercules fought as hard, wrenching Antaeus' arms, boxing his chest. Hercules seemed to be winning. Every time Antaeus weakened and lost his breath, Hercules threw him to the ground. Hercules did not know, however, that Antaeus got his strength from the earth, and that whenever Antaeus was in contact with the ground he was invincible. No man could hurt Antaeus while he was touching the earth.

Therefore, every time Hercules got the upper hand, Antaeus received his strength from the earth. The battle raged for most of the day, for Hercules was never able to deal the final blow.

As both wrestlers fought on into darkness, Hercules was losing strength. Just before the darkness prevented sight, Hercules flung Antaeus to the ground with one mighty heave. Antaeus lay there gasping, clutching the earth in his hands. Then he sprang up, ready to fight again.

Now Hercules knew Antaeus' secret. He shouted, "Antaeus, you shall die. No more will you touch the ground." With that Hercules, the mighty, muscled warrior lifted Antaeus high above his head, twisting his arms, and strangling the air from Antaeus' throat. With his legs flailing the leaves on the trees, high above the ground, Antaeus struggled for his life. But there was no hope. With one last mighty twist, Hercules strangled Antaeus to death.

That battle had caused the trees to lose their leaves, the road was a welter of dust, and the sounds of the struggle echoed off the mountains. The great Antaeus, the man of the earth, was dead. The temple roof of skulls would never be finished.

Hercules, the great hero, picked up Antaeus' body, flung it off the road, and continued his way home.

Antaeus

Borden Deal

In this story T. J.'s strength, like that of Antaeus, comes from the soil.

This was during the wartime, when lots of people were coming North for jobs in factories and war industries, when people moved around a lot more than they do now and sometimes kids were thrown into new groups and new lives that were completely different from anything they had ever known before. I remember this one kid; T. J. his name was, from somewhere down

South, whose family moved into our building during that time. They'd come North with everything they owned piled into the back seat of an old-model sedan that you wouldn't expect could make the trip, with T. J. and his three younger sisters riding shakily atop the load of junk.

Our building was just like all the others there, with families crowded into a few rooms, and I guess there were twenty-five or thirty kids about my age in that one building. Of course, there were a few of us who formed a gang and ran together all the time after school, and I was the one who brought T. J. in and started the whole thing.

The building right next door to us was a factory where they made walking dolls. It was a low building with a flat, tarred roof that had a parapet all around it about head-high, and we'd found out a long time before that no one, not even the watchman, paid any attention to the roof because it was higher than any of the other buildings around. So my gang used the roof as a headquarters. We could get up there by crossing over to the fire escape from our own roof on a plank and then going on up. It was a secret place for us, where nobody else could go without our permission.

I remember the day I first took T. J. up there to meet the gang. He was a stocky, robust kid with a shock of white hair, nothing sissy about him except his voice—he talked different from any of us, and you noticed it right away. But I liked him anyway, so I told him to come on up.

We climbed up over the parapet and dropped down on the roof. The rest of the gang were already there.

"Hi," I said. I jerked my thumb at T. J. "He just moved into the building yesterday."

He just stood there, not scared or anything, just looking, like the first time you see somebody you're not sure you're going to like.

"Hi," Blackie said. "Where you from?"

"Marion County," T. J. said.

We laughed. "Marion County?" I said. "Where's that?"

He looked at me like I was a stranger, too. "It's in Alabama," he said, like I ought to know where it was.

"What's your name?" Charley said.

"T. J.," he said, looking back at him. He had pale blue eyes that looked washed-out, but he looked directly at Charley, waiting for his reaction. He'll be all right, I thought. No sissy in him . . . except that voice. Who ever talked like that?

"T. J.," Blackie said. "That's just initials. What's your real name? Nobody in the world has just initials."

"I do," he said. "And they're T. J. That's all the name I got."

His voice was resolute with the knowledge of his rightness, and for a moment no one had anything to say. T. J. looked around at the rooftop and down at the black tar under his feet. "Down yonder where I come from," he said, "we played out in the woods. Don't you-all have no woods around here?"

"Naw," Blackie said. "There's the park a few blocks over, but it's full of kids and cops and old women. You can't do a thing."

T. J. kept looking at the tar under his feet. "You mean you ain't got no fields to raise nothing in? No watermelons or nothing?"

"Naw," I said scornfully. "What do you want to grow something for? The folks can buy everything they need at the store."

He looked at me again with that strange, unknowing look. "In Marion County," he said, "I had my own acre of cotton and my own acre of corn. It was mine to plant ever' year."

He sounded like it was something to be proud of, and in some obscure way it made the rest of us angry. "Heck!" Blackie said. "Who'd want to have their own acre of cotton and corn? That's just work. What can you do with an acre of cotton and corn?"

T. J. looked at him. "Well, you get part of the bale offen your acre," he said seriously. "And I fed my acre of corn to my calf."

We didn't really know what he was talking about, so we were more puzzled than angry; otherwise, I guess, we'd have chased him off the roof and wouldn't let him be part of our gang. But he was strange and different, and we were all attracted by his stolid sense of rightness and belonging, maybe by the strange softness of his voice contrasting our own tones of speech into harshness.

He moved his foot against the black tar. "We could make our own field right here," he said softly, thoughtfully. "Come spring we could raise us what we want to . . . watermelons and garden truck and no telling what all."

"You'd have to be a good farmer to make these tar roofs grow any watermelons," I said. We all laughed.

But T. J. looked serious. "We could haul us some dirt up here," he said. "And spread it out even and water it, and before you know it, we'd have us a crop in here." He looked at us intently. "Wouldn't that be fun?"

"They wouldn't let us," Blackie said quickly.

"I thought you said this was you-all's roof," T. J. said to me. "That you-all could do anything you wanted up here."

"They've never bothered us," I said. I felt the idea beginning to catch fire in me. It was a big idea, and it took a while for it to sink in, but the more I thought about it, the better I liked it. "Say," I said to the gang, "he might have something there. Just make us a regular roof garden, with flowers and grass and trees and everything. And all ours, too," I said. "We wouldn't let anybody up here except the ones we wanted to."

"It'd take a while to grow trees," T. J. said quickly, but we weren't paying any attention to him. They were all talking about it suddenly, all excited with the idea after I'd put it in the way they could catch hold of it. Only rich people had roof gardens, we knew, and the idea of our own private domain excited them.

"We could bring it up in sacks and boxes," Blackie said. "We'd have to do it while the folks weren't paying any attention to us. We'd have to come up to the roof of our building and then cross over with it."

"Where could we get the dirt?" somebody said worriedly.

"Out of those vacant lots over close to school," Blackie said. "Nobody'd notice if we scraped it up."

I slapped T. J. on the shoulder. "Man, you had a wonderful idea," I said, and everybody grinned at him, remembering he had started it. "Our own private roof garden."

He grinned back. "It'll be ourn," he said. "All ourn." Then he looked thoughtful again. "Maybe I can lay my hands on some cotton seed, too. You think we could raise us some cotton?"

We'd started big projects before at one time or another, like any gang of kids, but they'd always petered out for lack of organization and direction. But this one didn't . . . somehow or other T. J. kept it going all through the winter months. He kept talking about the watermelons and the cotton we'd raise, come spring, and when even that wouldn't work, he'd switch around to my idea of flowers and grass and trees, though he was always honest enough to add that it'd take a while to get any trees started. He always had it on his mind, and he'd mention it in school, getting them lined up to carry dirt that afternoon, saying in a casual way that he reckoned a few more weeks ought to see the job through.

Our little area of private earth grew slowly. T. J. was smart enough to start in one corner of the building, heaping up the carried earth two or three feet thick, so that we had an immediate result to look at, to contemplate with awe. Some of the evenings T. J. alone was carrying earth up to the building, the rest of the gang distracted by other enterprises or interests, but T. J. kept plugging along on his own, and eventually we'd all come back to him again, and then our own little acre would grow more rapidly.

He was careful about the kind of dirt he'd let us carry up there, and more than once he dumped a sandy load over the parapet into the areaway below because it wasn't good enough. He found out the kinds of earth in all the vacant lots for blocks around. He'd pick it up and feel it and smell it, frozen though it was sometimes, and then he'd say it was good growing soil or it wasn't worth anything and we'd have to go on somewhere else.

Thinking about it now, I don't see how he kept us at it. It was hard work, lugging paper sacks and boxes of dirt all the way up the stairs of our own building, keeping out of the way of the grownups so they wouldn't catch on to what we were doing. They probably wouldn't have cared, for they didn't pay much attention to us, but we wanted to keep it secret anyway. Then we had to go through the trap door to our roof, teeter over a plank to the fire escape, then climb two or three stories to the parapet and drop down onto the roof. All that for a small pile of earth that sometimes didn't seem worth the effort. But T. J. kept the vision bright within us, his words shrewd and calculated toward the fulfillment of his dream; and he worked harder than any of us. He seemed driven toward a goal that we couldn't see, a particular point in time that would be definitely marked by signs and wonders that only he could see.

The laborious earth just lay there during the cold months, inert and lifeless, the clods lumpy and cold under our feet when we walked over it. But one day it rained, and afterward there was a softness in the air and the earth was alive and giving again with moisture and warmth. That evening T. J. smelled the air, his nostrils dilating with the odor of the earth under his feet.

"It's spring," he said, and there was a gladness rising in his voice that filled us all with the same feeling. "It's mighty late for it, but it's spring. I'd just about decided it wasn't never gonna get here at all."

We were all sniffing at the air, too, trying to smell it the way that T. J. did, and I can still remember the sweet odor of the earth under our feet. It was the first time in my life that spring and spring earth had meant anything to me. I looked at T. J. then, knowing in a faint way the hunger within him through the toilsome winter months, knowing the dream that lay behind his plan. He was a new Antaeus, preparing his own bed of strength.

"Planting time," he said. "We'll have to find us some seed."

"What do we do?" Blackie said. "How do we do it?"

"First we'll have to break up the clods," T. J. said. "That won't be hard to do. Then we plant the seed, and after a while they come up. Then you got you a crop." He frowned. "But you ain't got it raised yet. You got to tend it and hoe it and take care of it, and all the time it's growing and growing while you're awake and while you're asleep. Then you lay it by when it's growed and let it ripen, and then you got you a crop."

"There's those wholesale seed houses over on Sixth," I said. "We could probably swipe some grass seed over there."

T. J. looked at the earth. "You-all seem mighty set on raising some grass," he said. "I ain't never put no effort into that. I spent all my life trying not to raise grass."

"But it's pretty," Blackie said. "We could play on it and take sunbaths on it. Like having our own lawn. Lots of people got lawns."

"Well," T. J. said. He looked at the rest of us, hesitant for the first time. He kept on looking at us for a moment. "I did have it in mind to raise some corn and vegetables. But we'll plant grass."

He was smart. He knew where to give in. And I don't suppose it made any difference to him really. He just wanted to grow something, even if it was grass.

"Of course," he said, "I do think we ought to plant a row of watermelons. They'd be mighty nice to eat while we was a-laying on that grass."

We all laughed. "All right," I said. "We'll plant us a row of watermelons."

Things went very quickly then. Perhaps half the roof was covered with the earth, the half that wasn't broken by ventilators, and we swiped pocketfuls of grass seed from the open bins in the wholesale seed house, mingling among the buyers on Saturdays and during the school lunch hour. T. J. showed us how to prepare the earth, breaking up the clods and smoothing it and sowing the grass seed. It looked rich and black now with moisture, receiving of the seed, and it seemed that the grass sprang up overnight, pale green in the early spring.

We couldn't keep from looking at it, unable to believe that we had created this delicate growth. We looked at T. J. with understanding now, knowing the fulfillment of the plan he had carried alone within his mind. We had worked without full understanding of the task, but he had known all the time.

We found that we couldn't walk or play on the delicate blades, as we had expected to, but we didn't mind. It was enough just to look at it, to realize that it was the work of our own hands, and each evening the whole gang was there, trying to measure the growth that had been achieved that day.

One time a foot was placed on the plot of ground . . . one time only, Blackie stepping onto it with sudden bravado. Then he looked at the crushed blades, and there was shame in his face. He did not do it again. This was his grass, too, and not to be desecrated. No one said anything, for it was not necessary.

T. J. had reserved a small section for watermelons, and he was still trying to find some seed for it. The wholesale house didn't have any watermelon seed, and we didn't know where we could lay our hands on them. T J. shaped the earth into mounds, ready to receive them, three mounds lying in a straight line along the edge of the grass plot.

We had just about decided that we'd have to buy the seed if we were to get them. It was a violation of our principles, but we were anxious to get the watermelons started. Somewhere or other, T. J. got his hands on a seed catalogue and brought it one evening to our roof garden.

"We can order them now," he said, showing us the catalogue. "Look!"

We all crowded around, looking at the fat, green watermelons pictured in full color on the pages. Some of them were split open, showing the red, tempting meat, making our mouths water.

"Now we got to scrape up some seed money," T. J. said, looking at us. "I got a quarter. How much you-all got?"

We made up a couple of dollars between us, and T. J. nodded his head. "That'll be more than enough. Now we got to decide what kind to get. I think them Kleckley Sweets. What do you-all think?"

He was going into esoteric matters beyond our reach. We hadn't even known there were different kinds of melons. So we just nodded our heads and agreed that yes, we thought the Kleckley Sweets too.

"I'll order them tonight," T. J. said. "We ought to have them in a few days."

Then an adult voice said behind us: "What are you boys doing up here?"

It startled us, for no one had ever come up here before, in all the time we had been using the roof of the factory. We jerked around and saw three men standing near the trap door at the other end of the roof. They weren't policemen, or night watchmen, but three men in plump business suits, looking at us. They walked toward us.

"What are you boys doing up here?" the one in the middle said again.

We stood still, guilt heavy among us, levied by the tone of voice, and looked at the three strangers.

The men stared at the grass flourishing behind us. "What's this?" the man said. "How did this get up here?"

"Sure is growing good, ain't it?" T. J. said conversationally. "We planted it."

The men kept looking at the grass as if they didn't believe it. It was a thick carpet over the earth now, a patch of deep greenness startling in the sterile industrial surroundings.

"Yes, sir," T. J. said proudly. "We toted that earth up here and planted that grass." He fluttered the seed catalogue. "And we're just fixing to plant us some watermelon."

The man looked at him then, his eyes strange and faraway. "What do you mean, putting this on the roof of my building?" he said. "Do you want to go to jail?"

T. J. looked shaken. The rest of us were silent, frightened by the authority of his voice. We had grown up aware of adult authority, of policemen and night watchmen and teachers, and this man sounded like all the others. But it was a new thing to T. J.

"Well, you wan't using the roof," T. J. said. He paused a moment and added shrewdly, "So we just thought to pretty it up a little bit."

"And sag it so I'd have to rebuild it," the man said sharply. He turned away, saying to a man beside him, "See that all that junk is shoveled off by tomorrow."

"Yes, sir," the man said.

T. J. started forward. "You can't do that," he said. "We toted it up here, and it's our earth. We planted it and raised it and toted it up here."

The man stared at him coldly. "But it's my building," he said. "It's to be shoveled off tomorrow."

"It's our earth," T. J. said desperately. "You ain't got no right!"

The men walked on without listening and descended clumsily through the trap door. T. J. stood looking after them, his body tense with anger, until they had disappeared. They wouldn't even argue with him, wouldn't let him defend his earth-rights.

He turned to us. "We won't let 'em do it," he said fiercely. "We'll stay up here all day tomorrow and the day after that, and we won't let 'em do it."

We just looked at him. We knew that there was no stopping it. He saw it in our faces, and his face wavered for a moment before he gripped it into determination.

"They ain't got no right," he said. "It's our earth. It's our land. Can't nobody touch a man's own land."

We kept on looking at him, listening to the words but knowing that it was no use. The adult world had descended on us even in our richest dream, and we knew there was no calculating the adult world, no fighting it, no winning against it.

We started moving slowly toward the parapet and the fire escape, avoiding a last look at the green beauty of the earth that T. J. had planted for us . . . had planted deeply in our minds as well as in our experience. We filed slowly over the edge and down the steps to the plank, T. J. coming last, and all of us could feel the weight of his grief behind us.

"Wait a minute," he said suddenly, his voice harsh with the effort of calling. We stopped and turned, held by the tone of his voice, and looked up at him standing above us on the fire escape.

"We can't stop them?" he said, looking down at us, his face strange in the dusky light. "There ain't no way to stop 'em?"

"No," Blackie said with finality. "They own the building."

We stood still for a moment, looking up at T. J., caught into inaction by the decision working in his face. He stared back at us, and his face was pale and mean in the poor light, with a bald nakedness in his skin like cripples have sometimes.

"They ain't gonna touch my earth," he said fiercely. "They ain't gonna lay a hand on it! Come on."

He turned around and started up the fire escape again, almost running against the effort of climbing. We followed more slowly, not knowing what he intended. By the time we reached him, he had seized a board and thrust it into the soil, scooping it up and flinging it over the parapet into the areaway below. He straightened and looked us squarely in the face.

"They can't touch it," he said. "I won't let 'em lay a dirty hand on it!"

We saw it then. He stooped to his labor again and we followed, the gusts of his anger moving in frenzied labor among us as we scattered along the edge of earth, scooping it and throwing it over the parapet, destroying with anger the growth we had nurtured with such tender care. The soil carried swiftly into the dark areaway, the green blades of grass crumpled and twisted in the falling.

It took less time than you would think . . . the task of destruction is infinitely easier than that of creation. We stopped at the end, leaving only a scattering of loose soil, and when it was finally over, a stillness stood among the group and over the factory building. We looked down at the bare sterility of black tar, felt the harsh texture of it under the soles of our shoes, and the anger had gone out of us, leaving only a sore aching in our minds like over-stretched muscles.

T. J. stooped for a moment, his breathing slowing

from anger and effort, caught into the same contemplation of destruction as all of us. He stooped slowly, finally, and picked up a lonely blade of grass left trampled under our feet and put it between his teeth, tasting it, sucking the greenness out of it into his mouth. Then he started walking toward the fire escape, moving before any of us were ready to move, and disappeared over the edge while we stared after him.

We followed him, but he was already halfway down to the ground, going on past the board where we crossed over, climbing down into the areaway. We saw the last section swing down with his weight, and then he stood on the concrete below us, looking at the small pile of anonymous earth scattered by our throwing. Then he walked across the place where we could see him and disappeared toward the street without glancing back, without looking up to see us watching him.

They did not find him for two weeks. Then the Nashville police caught him just outside the Nashville freight yards. He was walking along the railroad track; still heading south, still heading home.

As for us, who had no remembered home to call us . . . none of us ever again climbed the escape-way to the roof.

When I Heard the Learned Astronomer

When I heard the learn'd astronomer;
When the proofs, the figures, were ranged in columns
  before me;
When I was shown the charts and diagrams, to add,
  divide, and measure them;
When I, sitting, heard the astronomer, where he lectured
  with much applause in the lecture room,
How soon, unaccountable, I became tired and sick;
Till rising and gliding out, I wander'd off by myself,
In the mystical moist night-air, and from time to time,
Look'd up in perfect silence at the stars.

Walt Whitman

All Nature Sings!

J. Gresham Machen

As our cities spread rapidly in every direction, and as the pace of living becomes more and more hurried, people feel increasingly the need of the quietude of nature. Dr. Machen, a distinguished scholar and teacher, found not only rest but also revelation in the mountains of Europe and America.

The testimony of nature to nature's God comes to men in different ways. To some it speaks most clearly through the knowledge of nature possessed by the scientist. To others it comes by what the poet Browning calls "a sunset touch." To one man in one way, to another in another.

To me nature speaks most clearly in the majesty and beauty of the hills. One day in the summer of 1932 I stood on the summit of the Matterhorn in the Alps. Some people can stand there and see very little. Depreciating the Matterhorn is a recognized part of modern books on mountain climbing. The great mountain, it is said, has been sadly spoiled. Why, you can even see sardine cans on those rocks that so tempted the ambition of climbers in Whymper's day.

Well, I can only say that I do not remember seeing a single can when I stood on the Matterhorn. Perhaps that was partly because of the unusual masses of fresh snow which were then on the mountain; but I think it was also due to the fact that unlike some people I had eyes for something else. I saw the vastness of the Italian plain, which was like a symbol of infinity. I saw the snows of distant mountains. I saw the sweet green valleys far, far below, at my feet. I saw the whole glorious round of glittering peaks, bathed in an unearthly light. And as I see that glorious vision again before me now, I am thankful from the bottom of my heart that from my mother's knee I have known to whom all that glory is due.

Then I love the softer beauties of nature also. I wonder whether you love them with me. Some years ago, in the White Mountains, I walked beside a brook. I have seen, I suppose, hundreds of brooks. But somehow I remember particularly that one. I am not going to tell you where it is, because if I did you might write to the National Park Service about it and get them to put a scenic highway along it, and then it would be forever ruined. But when I walked along it, it was untouched. I cherish the memory of it. It was gentle and sweet and lovely beyond all words. I think a man might travel through all the world and never see anything lovelier than a White Mountain brook. Very wonderful is the variety of nature in her changing moods.

Silence too, the silence of nature, can be a very revealing thing. I remember one day when I spent a peaceful half-hour in the sunlight on the summit of a mountain in the Franconia range. I there experienced something very rare. Would you believe it, my friends? It was really *silent* on that sunny mountain top. There was not the honk of a motor horn; there was no jazz music; there was not even the rustling of the leaves. There was nothing but a strange, brooding silence. It was a precious time indeed. I shall never forget it all my life.

Please do not misunderstand me. I am not asking that everyone should love the beauties of nature as I love them. I well understand that there are many people who do not love the beauties of nature. Are they shut off from finding God revealed in the world that He has made?

That is not so, my friends; indeed, it is not so. The

mystery of the existence of the world presses itself upon different people in different ways. I remember, for example, a talk that I heard from a professor at an afternoon conference service many years ago. The professor said that he had had a friend who had come to a belief in God, or had come back to a belief in God, by—what do you suppose? Well, by a trip through Europe! As he went from city to city and observed the seething multitudes, the throngs upon throngs of men and women, somehow, he said, the conviction just seemed to come over him: "There is a God, there is a God."

Was that a foolish fancy? Were those experiences in my own life of which I have been bold enough to speak merely meaningless dreams? Or were they true testimonies to something marvelous beyond? Were they moments when God was graciously revealing Himself to me through the glory of the world that He has made?

A Christian ought not to be afraid to give the latter answer. The revelation of God through nature has the stamp of approval put upon it by the Bible. The Bible clearly teaches that nature reveals the glory of God.

In a wonderful passage in the first chapter of the Epistle to the Romans the Apostle Paul says that "the invisible things of him from the creation of the world are clearly seen, being understood by the things that are made, even his eternal power and Godhead." Here the Bible approves the arguments of those who in systematic fashion argue from the existence of the world to the existence of a divine Maker of the world.

But the Bible also approves those more unreasoned flashes of knowledge in which suddenly we see God's workmanship in the beauty and the majesty of His world. "The heavens declare the glory of God; and the firmament sheweth his handiwork," says the Psalmist.

And what said our Lord Jesus Christ. "Even Solomon in all his glory," said He of the lilies of the field, "was not arrayed like one of these."

All that is true. The revelation of God through nature is a very precious thing. But then a serious question arises. If God has revealed Himself through the things that He has made, why do so very few men listen to the revelation? The plain fact is that very few men arrive by a contemplation of nature at the true belief in a personal God. Even those scientists whose religious views are sometimes being incautiously welcomed by Christian people are often found upon closer examination to believe only in a God who is identical with a spiritual purpose supposed to inhere in the world process itself and are found not to believe at all in a living and holy God, are found not to believe at all in the true God who created the heavens and the earth.

Why is that so? If God has revealed Himself so plainly through the world that He has made, why do men not see?

Well, when men do not see something, there are two possible explanations for the fact. One is that there is nothing there to see. The other is that the men who do not see are blind.

It is this latter explanation which the Bible gives for the failure of men to know God through the things that He has made. The Bible puts it very plainly in that same passage already quoted from the first chapter of Romans. "Their foolish heart," says Paul, "was darkened." Hence they did not see. The fault did not lie in nature. Men were "without excuse," Paul says, when they did not see what nature had to show. Their minds were blinded by sin.

That is a hard saying, but like many other hard

sayings it is true. We all of us, so long as we stand in our own right, and have not had our eyes mysteriously opened, are lost and blind in sin.

The World Is Too Much with Us

The world is too much with us; late and soon,
Getting and spending, we lay waste our powers:
Little we see in Nature that is ours;
We have given our hearts away, a sordid boon!
This Sea that bares her bosom to the moon;
The winds that will be howling at all hours,
And are up-gathered now like sleeping flowers;
For this, for everything, we are out of tune;
It moves us not.—Great God! I'd rather be
A Pagan suckled in a creed outworn;
So might I, standing on this pleasant lea,
Have glimpses that would make me less forlorn;
Have sight of Proteus rising from the sea;
Or hear old Triton blow his wreathèd horn.

William Wordsworth

What are the circumstances that make the speaker prefer paganism? Do you agree with him?

A Song for Simplicity

There are some things that should be as they are:
plain, unadorned, common and all-complete;
things not in a clutter, not in a clump,
unmuddled and unmeddled with;
the straight, the smooth, the salt, the sour, the sweet.
For all that's timeless, untutored, untailored and un-
  tooled;
for innocence unschooled;
for unploughed prairies, primal snow and sod,
water unmuddied, wind unruled,
for these, thank God.

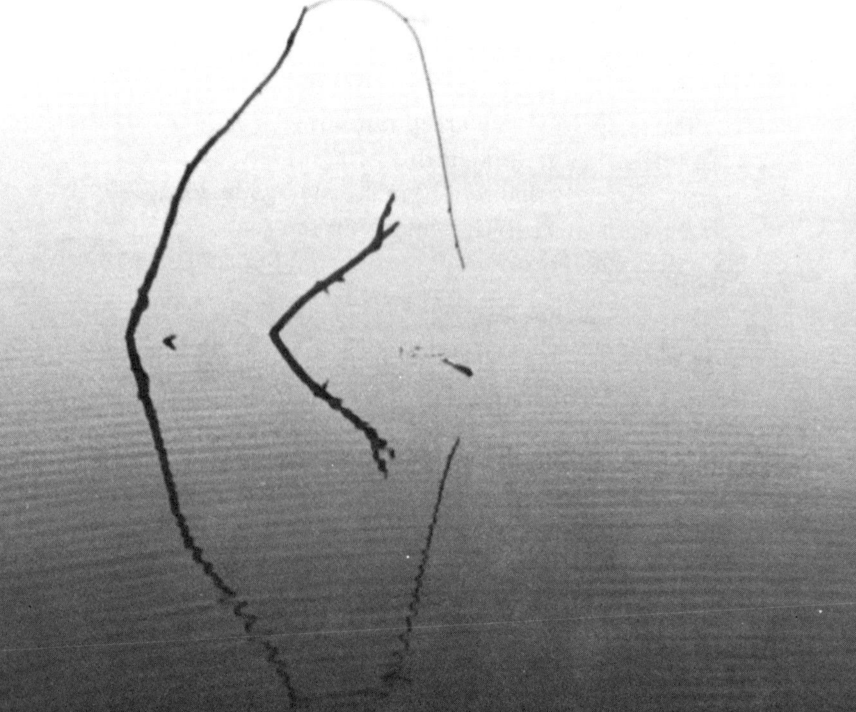

Singly and strongly, from each separate star
a brightness pricks the retina from far
to near. And for clear eyes to see
deep space and dark infinity
with an untroubled gaze,
give praise.

With both hands unjewelled and with unbound hair
beauty herself stands unselfconscious where
she is enough to have, and worth the always holding.
The mind perceiving her, the heart enfolding
echoes the unchanged pattern from above
that praises God for loveliness, and love.

Glory again to God for word and phrase
whose magic, matching the mind's computed leap,
lands on the lip of truth
(plain as a stone well's mouth, and as deep),
and for the drum, the bell, the flute, the harp, the bird,
for music, Praise! that speaks without a word.

As for the rightness to be found
in the unembellished square and the plain round,
in geometric statement of a curve
respond! without reserve
but with astonishment that there's for every man
one point of time, one plainly drafted plan,
and in your unique place
give glory for God's grace.

All this from him whose three-in-one
so simply brought to birth
from the red earth
a son.

All our complexity, diversity, decor
facet the gem, encrust the clarity.
So pierce you now the opalescent glaze
till all your praise
rises to him in whom you find no flaw.

Luci Shaw

Pied Beauty

Glory be to God for dappled things—
   For skies of couple-colour as a brinded cow;
      For rose-moles all in stipple upon trout that swim;
Fresh-firecoal chestnut-falls; finches' wings;
   Landscape plotted and pieced—fold, fallow, and
         plough;
      And all trades, their gear and tackle and trim.
All things counter, original, spare, strange;
   Whatever is fickle, freckled (who knows how?)
      With swift, slow; sweet, sour; adazzle, dim;
He fathers-forth whose beauty is past change:
               Praise him.

Gerard Manley Hopkins

This Land Is Your Land ©

This land is your land, this land is my land,
From California to the New York Island,
From the redwood forest to the gulf-stream waters,
This land was made for you and me.

As I went walking that ribbon of highway
I saw above me that endless skyway,
I saw below me that golden valley,
This land was made for you and me.

Chorus

I roamed and rambled, and I followed my footsteps,
To the sparkling sands of her diamond deserts,
All around me a voice was sounding,
This land was made for you and me.

Chorus

When the sun come shining, then I was strolling,
And the wheat fields waving, and the dust clouds
rolling,
A voice was chanting as the fog was lifting,
This land was made for you and me.

Chorus

Woody Guthrie